FLOATING

FLOATING

Hugo Leckey

DRAWINGS BY EUGENE LEE

W. W. NORTON & COMPANY

NEW YORK   LONDON

W. W. Norton & Company, Inc. 500 Fifth Avenue, New York, N.Y. 10110
W. W. Norton & Company Ltd. 37 Great Russell Street, London WC1B 3NU

Library of Congress Cataloging in Publication Data

Leckey, Hugo.
    Floating.

    1. Boat living.   I. Title.
GV777.7.L42   1982   643'.2   81–18735
ISBN 0 393 03272 8   AACR2

1 2 3 4 5 6 7 8 9 0

FOR

Stewart AND *Helen Harrison*

Contents

The beauty of the world has two edges,
one of laughter, one of anguish,
cutting the heart asunder.

—Virginia Woolf
A Room of One's Own

FLOATING

Floating

STAND ON A PIER. Perhaps a tall, spindle-legged, wooden pier in Maine where the tides rise and fall through two fathoms and more. The timbers are rough with splinters, the planking warped from the beating of sun and split from the insidious work of ice.

The coastline is rock-ribbed and the beaches are strewn with stones that builders use to shore up the pier. They pile stones within the rectangle formed by the pilings, and cage them with slats of wood so that the pier is supported and a breakwater is formed against the waves that fetch up under the power of the cold nor'easters that blow throughout the winter.

By good chance, the beach close to the pier is freed from rocks, and this allows for a dinghy tied to the pier to go gently aground in the muddy sand without damage, while fishermen can creep in or away on the very lip of the tide.

The feet of the pilings are likely clustered with

brown- and orange-tinted seaweed, and perhaps a few blue mussels that care for only a brief exposure to air cling there too. A little higher, some winkles or sea snails push their faces into the wood, and above them hangs a ring of green weed which stirs with the water's flow, although at low tide its delicate hair becomes matted and slimy to touch.

Around the half-tide mark, whitish crustaceans, barnacles, dwindle in number as they multiply upwards. They seem to me no earthly use at all, for, provided they receive enough sunlight to survive, they encrust rocks and lobster pots and the bottoms of boats. They are a menace, abrading bare feet and hands that contact the sharp rim of their tiny volcanic cones. They appear so soon at the faintest flaking of the antifoul paint on the bottom of a boat, and when they are scraped away, each shell breaks from its point of contact, leaving a tiny white image of its bite.

Children love piers. They love the perilous drop when the tide is out, down to the rocks and sand where clams may be spewing their silver streams of water in the air. They also love the more alarming wash and suck of waves that shake the pier when the tide is high. They climb about and fish, running back to the safety of land at a splash, or lying on their stomachs on a calm day, gazing into the strange magnification and refractions of clear, still water where a dinghy may be afloat.

The dinghy stirs and turns athwart, beads of water dropping from the loop of its painter. The paint has blistered on its dry hull, while its bottom, submerged

a few inches in the water, has a faint beard of weed
waving. The sun casts a shadow of the dinghy onto
the shell-littered sand a few dreamy feet below. The
boat slowly turns in air, and in water, and its shadow
moves darkly on the sand. And the child, lying quietly
on the pier, spies down the line of the painter to the
sure hardness of the hull, to the bottom of the boat
bulging underwater, and the mirage of the boat on
the sand.

The pier is hard and firm, the water soft, moving
even in its stillness, and the boat is floating, making a
bridge between the light warmth of air and the suste-
nance of water. To climb into that dinghy, to float
with fingers trailing in the water under the warm
sunlight, to feel the depth of the sea, would be to
know what floating is. But the child is called away,
distracted by parents calling from the shore; even so,
he carries with him the sense of another world.

There are three seas that press on our imaginations. They intertwine until image is colored with
image, letting us select whichever one we require,
whichever one we can contain.

The first sea is perhaps the kindest one, and surely
the most romantic. It is a sea celebrated in paintings
and poems. The storm-tossed bark making an offing
amidst spumes of wind-whipped waves crashing over
reefs. Its sails tear from the yardarms under a wind
that never ceases, while the reefs hunger for a fragile
hull that never arrives.

Here is a sea of tension and violence that disturbs,

but does no harm. Nor do the serene and cloud-colored celebrations of Turner, whose airy visions discover in a miraculous way that the stuff of water and of air belong to the same light. Wyeth sees the cast-off solitude of wetlands and abandoned skiffs. Coleridge presents the dank and parched vision of his "Ancient Mariner." Shakespeare sings Ariel's dolorous song, "Full fathom five my father lies."

Such seas haunt with danger and vibrate with the possibility of further life. But they are seas that neither ebb nor flow, and they do not warm or chill. They are caught only as imagined, and they have no scope beyond the edge of the canvas or the final stanza of the poem.

In some ways, these are the greatest seas of all, these wonders of imagination. For, although they are limited to their presentations, they speak of a scope that moves beyond experience toward the infinite being of the sea itself.

Then there is the sea we sail on. It is rough or smooth as winds affect it, riddled with currents, and deep depending on land masses. It wells high or low according to the moon and sun. We see it in light or darkness or fog. But we bring to our seeing of it our own emotional charge. The seasick sailor loathes the tempestuous heave that excites the racing sailor crowding on more sail. The solo circumnavigator may see the vast plains of oceans as a canvas on which to paint his own solitary way with a meditative joy, while the man shipwrecked and clinging to a raft sees a deadly silver lake that might as well be molten mercury. The cruising sailor looks to the sea in all weather as a medium through which to pass to his next safe port, while the saint finds in the flash of its reflecting surface an image of the infinite and of godhead.

But all of these people, all of whom come to the sea for diverse reasons, create their own sea to suit the purposes that took them to it. They are moved and cajoled and excited by seascape and visions. They are painters and poets who make for themselves through touch and sight and smell a dream of what their particular sea may be.

A sea described is a sea contained. That is what we do when we move from the sea of our imaginations to the sea we sail on. What we make bigger in our dreams we also reduce in our dreams. It is how we understand a world that is both dangerous to being and the source of being.

Lastly, there is the sea itself. It is made of chemicals and that particular combination of hydrogen and oxygen we call water. It is denser than air and covers most of Earth's surface, and boats float in it. Anything that falls into it is slowly destroyed, either by its fierce action of pounding or its corrosive nature. Between them they steal shape from what had shape and relentlessly work until everything is one. It cares for nothing, this sea, and is in its uncaring not unkind. It is simply itself. And if it is controlled at all, it is controlled by the sun, and not, as we generally think, by the moon who merely plays with it. For it is gathered by the sun into ice or released from ice at the polar caps so that there is more sea or less sea, and consequently more land or less land. It is the great nurturing mother of life, as the artist would say. And the scientist would agree that it cares for neither life nor death, being or nonbeing. It simply is.

How it delights us, this vast, cleansing, all-containing fluid. To swim in it, to take from it, to fathom and chart it, to watch it ebb and flow and see it rise in wrath or become balmy with calm. It is the most insinuating metaphor for the reaches of man's imagination. It is our way of knowing what has substance and what is without substance. On its moods we can model health and find the shape of evil.

Were the child to come back from his parents' call, were he to lie on the pier again, halfway between land and water, to see the dinghy that is in the water and out of the water, floating—surely, if he could speak, he would speak of his own conception. For we are created in water, curled up and thoughtlessly secure, safely anchored in that mothering harbor like a tiny ship in a pacific sea, nourished by the cord that ties us to . . . ah, but there lies the problem. We are born, and suffer our first wreck, being cast with a wave, bloody and terrified and helpless onto the land. We are born to flounder.

But to see a boat float, to climb into it and live between air and water, to be contained in all the earthy things that make a boat. Then in that sense of floating, that soft, lingering song where air and earth and water mingle, lies a gentle sense of eternal being.

The child is the artist and the dreamer and the unvanquished. He wants to come aboard and float.

Heating a Boat in New England

THE BEST HEAT of all is free, untroubled, tumbling sunlight, and New England is short of it.

The summer months are warm enough, and a few weeks in both spring and fall shimmer. The rest is cold and ice and worse, so that sailing is curtailed and boats are dumped up on land for two-thirds of the year. This seems a shame to me.

New England has some of the best cruising waters in the world, so good in fact that overcrowding in seaways and harbors is a problem second only to climate. But this is not true in the tag ends of the warm weather when tourists are gone, and anchorages are no longer cluttered with rafts of boats lying to a single anchor. After Labor Day, New England regains its familiar Yankee poise, and sailing is prime, provided one has heat.

Having a coal stove on board allows happy sailing for seven months of the year, for even in bad weather a good amount of chill can be suffered on deck with the thought of a warm dry cabin below. Dank clothes dry off quickly, sleeping bags are snug, while the notion of being the only boat lying in Cuttyhunk harbor in April or November, all comforts provided for below, makes my spine tingle.

A longer sailing season makes good economic sense. Even the wealthy admit that keeping a boat is expensive, which is perhaps why the word "yacht" has taken on such overtones of exclusivity and snobbishness. But the fact is that the expense of commissioning a boat for seven months is no greater than for three. The major expenses of hauling and painting are the same in both instances, while an idle boat is subject to terrible corrosion that is probably as expensive or worse than the extra cost for wear and tear a well-used boat will suffer. The longer the sailing season, the less expensive per hour of sailing your boat is. It is wonderful how the economics of things can be juggled, but from time to time I will do anything to have a boat.

A few years ago, when I purchased *Jabberwock,* a 32-foot steel sloop, I juggled one step further. I decided to live aboard her yearlong in New England waters so that, by not paying rent for a house, I could put that money into the boat and so afford her. This was the argument, not entirely sound, but one that pleased me at the time. Besides, I wanted to live on board all winter, in part to see what it would be like to have a floating home, what changes that small space would make on me and me on it, what pleasures and comfort could be gleaned from a mild craziness. The key to it was heat, and that concerned me.

I had been hanging around New England for several years, protected in steam-heated apartments and shielded by storm windows. The concept of dealing directly with snow and ice, for so living on a boat implied, frightened me. Ireland, where I was raised, can be raw and torturous, but rarely dangerous climatically, while Southern California where I had spent several years, spoils everyone. Even perfectly house-trained dogs around Los Angeles revert to the license of puppyhood on the odd occasion when rain sprinkles there. I had become such a California dog, staying indoors until the rain stopped, or using the car instead of an overcoat. Contemporary life had spoiled me.

I spent the summer searching for a boat, and acquired *Jabberwock* in September. Ironically I could have had her several months earlier, for she was the first suitable boat I looked at. But superstition got the best of me, and I refused to bid on her until I had seen several other craft.

What attracted me, in terms of living aboard, was the spacious simplicity of her cabin. The companionway led from the cockpit into a galley to port and a large chart table to starboard. This space was partially separated from the main cabin which had two ample berths. Beyond was a large hanging locker and enclosed head, and in the forward cabin were comfortable V-berths. There was headroom throughout, which seemed essential when considering winter quarters. Furthermore, the cabin sole was shallow, allowing one to peer readily out of doghouse windows and portholes. There was a breezy open feeling in her design that appealed to me as unclaustrophobic and bright. She was built in Holland, and she carried about her that simple, uncluttered quality of a Vermeer interior.

I had in mind to heat her with a stove, a little pot-belly stove that would burn coal, and could be installed by removing a berth in the main cabin, allowing space for the addition of a fixed table which the sloop lacked. Eventually these things came to fruition in a form I had not quite imagined. And this is close to the essence of boats and boating. Everything will likely happen, but never quite as one expects it to.

There was a flurry of hurricanes that season, one of which came charging toward New England before veering east and passing harmlessly to sea beyond Nantucket. Thereafter the fall was kindly and warm, one of the long, drawn-out Indian summers so often recorded in books, so rarely seen. Perhaps it is the memory of a few warm days that make an Indian summer. Perhaps they do not exist at all.

The sailing was pleasant, and I was often joined by my friends Eugene and Franne Lee who were themselves interested in buying a boat to live on. We cruised around Narragansett Bay in Rhode Island, looking for a likely spot to winter *Jabberwock,* for at this time she was lying on a mooring belonging to the Lees in nearby East Greenwich Bay.

I by far prefer to live on a boat moored or anchored off. It is then she turns with wind and tide, and the quiet comfort of the cabin at night with the oil lamps twinkling seems most profound. There is, unfortunately, a price to pay, for it is very difficult to get work done on a boat without running water, electrical current for power tools, and dock space. It is even more difficult (although perhaps I mean foolish) to be seen dressed up for a Governor's reception at The State House while rowing ashore in a rain squall and surrounded by a group of yachts racing. That is summer stuff.

We settled finally for a berth in a marina on the Pawtuxet River that feeds into Narragansett Bay near Providence. The marina lies about a quarter of a mile upstream, well protected from seas, while the village on a hill above the river blunts the north wind that prevails during winter.

Meanwhile I kept warm enough on board. Evenings got chilly, but cooking on the alcohol stove provided heat, as did the three brass kerosene lamps. But when rain came, the boat swirled with dampness, a pervasive cold that even thick sweaters failed to keep at bay.

At first I kept the alcohol stove burning with a very low flame, an inverted clay pot set over it. The pot acted as a radiator and provided a pleasant glow more conducive to heating than burning the flame naked and allowing heat to rise to the cabin roof where it escaped swiftly through the ventilators. This is a useful heat source on a foggy day if a boat lacks a heating stove, although there are drawbacks. Stove alcohol is as expensive to burn as its brother is to drink, while that glowing pot is all too easily fingered with painful results. The instability of the pot makes this method useless in any sort of sea.

Once October advanced, temperatures began dropping seriously. After a night when life ground down to 39 degrees, I bought an electric heater, good only for dockside use where power is available. This was a conventional machine, slender bands of metal getting red-hot, heat being pushed forward by an interior fan. It had a thermostat and could maintain a given temperature, and it had the advantage of switching itself off when tipped over accidentally. I felt good about leaving it going when I was ashore, and for the time being I was warm enough, even with the lingering threats of local boatmen whose unified forecast was one uncompromising line: You'll freeze to death.

Looking back on it, my only real worry was that *Jabberwock,* being built of steel, would be such a conductor of cold that the amount of heat required for comfort and survival might be more than I could produce. I used to wander around the cabin, feeling the temperature of the hull beneath and above the waterline. It always felt as cold as any stone.

On this I speculated. For instance, the marina had a bubbling system to keep the line of docked boats free of ice. A bubbling system is simple and effective.

Perforated air hoses are laid under water, the hoses running up and down the line of docked boats. When temperatures drop low enough to start the formation of ice, compressed air is pumped through these hoses. The air escapes through the perforations and bubbles up to the surface. This does two things to prevent water from turning into ice. It stirs up the relatively warm water below, thus warming the colder layer of surface water, while the constant boiling motion of the bubbles breaks the surface tension and impedes the formation of ice.

Since water freezes at 32 degrees, I reckoned this would be the severest degree of cold I would have to deal with below the waterline. Strictly speaking this is not quite the case, since impure and saline water, particularly in turbulence, can drop well below the freezing point without ice forming. But compared to the minus degrees of cold I was anticipating above the waterline, such icy water seemed like a warm muff.

By and large the bubbling system worked. But unfortunately the machine that drove compressed air through the hoses often did not. The machine was a big rusty blunderbuss of a compressor, driven by a cantankerous, smoke-belching gasoline engine, and, as you might expect, when the really cold snaps arrived, the engine often failed to start. This is the nature of things mechanical.

Ice began to form, at first a black skim that became opaque and white as it thickened, imperceptibly encroaching on the circle of water the boat floated in. The boat's small motions from tidal changes, wind, and the river's current helped keep the final couple of feet free from the cloying sheet of glass. But on it came, until one bright morning I came on deck and found ice fastened to the hull.

There is an insanely abandoned sense when one hops over the stern pulpit and strolls casually around the outside of a floating boat. The sun shone coldly from an azure sky. The white ice was tight against the blue hull. On land the marina operator cursed and poured ether into the maw of his machine. There was nothing to do but wait for a thaw. I wandered off across the water and up to Pawtuxet village for some hot coffee. At worst the ice would scrape a little paint away.

Up in Maine, where people are as hardy as they come, wintering schooners are sometimes left swinging with the wind and tides in some sheltered anchorage. In all but the most ferocious cold, the boat's constant motion keeps it ice-free. The danger is not so much from being ice-bound, but from the damage that hull and anchor rode can suffer from sheets and chunks of ice floating free and bashing into the hull. Often boats can be reasonably protected from such damage by fixing strong planking around the entire waterline. But the enormous weight and drag of an ice pack breaking up and pressing on the hull can pluck out the strongest mooring.

By the time November rolled along, *Jabberwock* had been covered by a wooden frame stretched with clear heavy plastic. This protected her decks and cockpit from snow and ice, and made a comforting pocket of air that helped to insulate her topsides. But still no stove.

The problem was that I didn't really know how to proceed. The appropriate stove had not revealed itself, and there was to come the difficult business of installing it by ripping out a berth and significantly rebuilding the cabin. I recalled an ancient professor from whom I learned but one thing—he said that he rarely went to the library to discover a point of information he lacked. Instead he would merely ask his friends for the answer. I thought.this cogent advice, so I got on the phone and called Eugene and Franne Lee.

It happens that the Lees are designers of theatrical sets and costumes, and they have an amazing ability to solve all manner of practical problems. When I said, Help, I'm getting cold, Eugene reasonably suggested, Let's go buy a stove.

Sometimes what is needed is a little effort. That very evening we came across a Shipmate stove. These stoves are similar in design to the traditional wood-burning kitchen stoves used for cooking, baking and heating, but the Shipmate is a minature version, designed specifically for boats. This was a Shipmate 211, a cast-iron stove that was beautiful to look at. Perhaps its miniaturization made it so extraordinarily appealing, or perhaps my happy vision of heat descended on it. But I loved it, called it "Stovie," and bought it on the spot for a hundred dollars.

On its left side was a brick-lined firebox with a door for adding coal and a lower door for raking out ashes.

On its right was a tiny oven, in which a year later I baked an appropriately tiny turkey for Thanksgiving. On top were two hot plates and an outlet for the stovepipe. It was simple and its tiny parts radiated such authority it seemed a work of art.

Away went all notion of a potbelly stove. Here was a model good for cooking as well as for heat, while the design was thoughtful of sailing problems. The stove top was surrounded by fiddles and clamps to holds pots in place in a sea, and the size seemed perfect. How much it weighed I don't know, but the three of us were hard put loading it into the car, and that was nothing compared to carrying it down the wobbling floating docks which happened to be slick with ice that night. The little black beast must have weighed close to 100 pounds, no easy heft to toss on board and balance down the companionway.

We perched the stove on the starboard berth where it looked alarmingly big, but Franne pointed out that once the berth was lowered it would seem less big by half. After long debate, we agreed the stove should face to port, allowing the firebox door to open into the aisle. I would have preferred the stove athwartships, for I had a frightening image of being under sail on the starboard tack and glancing down the companionway to see a spew of redhot coals fly from an open firebox. This was such a pervasive fantasy that I took precautions to insure against this particular disaster. I purchased a couple of metal springs with hooks on both ends, and secured them about the

body of the stove so that the springs clamped the doors decisively shut.

In a couple of days, the berth was torn out, and the stove temporarily placed on plywood about four inches above the cabin sole. This would be its permanent position, so the next step was to get it vented.

I have mentioned that *Jabberwock* was made of steel, steel so beautifully rolled and worked that she looked more like a fiberglass boat. The doghouse and cabin were also steel, and, some way or other, a stovepipe had to get through that roof. It happens I have a great respect for steel—the very word conjures up armor, lances, lethal swords—and the idea of cutting through a steel hull, even above the waterline, seemed paralyzing. Wood is a workable idea, gold malleable, but steel is immutable.

No so. Eugene measured, sketched, and with a drill and bit shrieked out a hole into which the slender jiggling blade of a saw would fit. Two broken blades later, there was a five-inch-diameter hole in the cabin roof.

The local hardware store supplied the necessary lengths of galvanized stovepipe, which we connected up and topped with a little tin hat to keep the rain out. A few handfuls of charcoal, some starter fluid, a match, and wisps of smoke drifted up by the mast. Heat, survival, perpetual soups—for what is a stove better for than the slow, gentle heat that provokes soups into their concentrated and healthful essence? It was a euphoric beginning, especially when a friend stepped into the cockpit five minutes after the stove was lighted, and swore he could feel the heat outside. Perhaps he could. The idea of a stove is sometimes as warming as the heat one gets from it.

I was content and blithely ignorant, for I had no notion that it would be three months before the carpentry was finished at a cost of 800 dollars, or that I yet had to learn about the stove the hard way.

Fuel and how to fruitfully use it became my major concern. I began by burning charcoal briquets. They ignited readily, produced a wondrous number of calories, and disappeared. Even with the dampers closed, the draught was such that a full firebox of charcoal burned in a couple of hours. It was expensive and had no staying power.

This need to be frequently tending the fire was no good at all. The only way I could afford *Jabberwock* was by working. That meant I had to be ashore before nine in the morning and often didn't return until eight at night. I needed fuel to slumber along for twelve hours. Coal, I thought, would do the trick.

I had been brought up in houses heated by coal. The technique I recalled from my childhood which gave a fire an overnight chance was to build up a good heart of hot coals and then "damp it down" by covering the hot coals with "slack," a fine pebbly coal. The slack had a smothering effect while slowly igniting itself. This, in a good fireplace, would see a fire mildly through the night, and in the morning the coals could be poked into a fresh flame before the addition of fuel. I was all confidence in this instance.

Coal for home use is sold in several sizes—pea coal,

chestnut coal and cannel coal. As you might expect, the lumps of coal are more or less pea-sized, chestnut-sized, while cannel coal is more oily and comes in large hunks six to ten inches in size. It is reported to produce the hottest coal fire possible.

In Rhode Island there was only one place left to purchase coal, "The People's Coal Company." It was run by a kindly, disorganized man who liked to talk to me about the therapeutic value of coal. Watching it glow and flicker, he said, is pacifying and good for the soul. I believed him, and enjoyed poking around the coal yard. There were railroad tracks curving through large yards where the coal in great stacks slithered mountainously over itself. The coal was sold in 50-pound amounts, rather improbably contained in heavy paper sacks.

The little shop where business was conducted on stray bits of paper and torn carbon copies was disappointingly heated by radiators, but it contained all manner of stoves, screens, fire irons—the paraphernalia of coal burning, all of which became extremely interesting to me. I bought a coal scuttle—everything was a bargain at "The People's Coal Company"—and it turned out this contained enough fuel to keep the fire going for a day. I had not sufficient room on *Jabberwock* to build in a coal bin, and had to keep sacks of coal sitting in the covered cockpit during winter.

I began with 200 pounds of chestnut coal. It did not work. That is to say, I could not make it burn. I started it with paper and kindling, added coal which began to burn, and, just when things were getting warm, the coal went out. No amount of fiddling with draughts seemed to brighten the diminishing red heart. The fire went out, the frost began to creep, and I resorted to charcoal. I decided that the size of chestnut coal in such a small firebox was the problem. The pore spaces between the lumps of coal were perhaps too large in such a confined firebox, so that a few burning coals failed to generate enough heat to ignite their brothers.

The following day I carted the 200 pounds of chestnut coal back down the wobbling, snowy, floating docks, across the parking lot and into my station wagon. Back to "The People's Coal Company." The owner was sympathetic and convinced me a hotter coal might do the trick. He sold me a trial bag of cannel coal. Of course it came in big lumps, but he explained that it could be easily shaled by the blow of a hammer.

There was about me at this time a desperation that the stove was failing. Charcoal was effective for only brief periods of heat, and if I was to winter aboard successfully, considering sleep and onshore work demands, a better solution had to be found.

For reasons of meetings and a cocktail party, it was close to ten that night before I staggered down the treacherous dock lugging a 50-pound bag of cannel coal. The boat was frigid when I came on board, the little electric heater blasting away like an organ without wind.

I'm not sure why I failed to consider the more importunate aspects of hammering coal into small fragments on a boat. I admit to a certain flaw in my character whereby things that seem so good and solid in this world, like "Stovie," deserve unalloyed support, even in the jaws of failure. If she needed cannel coal, she would have it.

Without removing my good overcoat, or changing from city clothes and shoes, I picked up a hammer and blattered a little drunkenly at the big, oily hunks of coal. It shaled indeed, and powdered too, while sharp splinters flew about the interior of the cabin. I was nothing but hope, and joyous with the information that cannel coal would light up in a flash.

It did not. It began to burn, and faltered, while I lounged by, fully clad, hungry, and exasperated enough to grab a can of charcoal lighter fluid and squirt it over the sullen black coals. That failed to ignite and as I watched a billow of gaseous fumes drift up, in my wisdom I lighted a match and threw it into the firebox.

Whuuuump! As my body landed on the port berth, I remember thinking with absolute clarity, Smother it. I grabbed a blanket and wrapped my burning head tight, the bitter reek of burned hair already in my nostrils. Once I was extinguished, the terror hit me. Had I set the boat on fire? I jumped up and saw the stove roaring. Tongues of yellow flame were leaping out of the firebox, around the oven and up the stovepipe. I got the hot plate on and still could see these fearsome tongues through cracks and seams never observed before. I restricted the draught intake, and ran on deck, fearful that the mast or the plastic cover might be on fire.

Fortunately the flames had not leaped up the entire stovepipe. But spewing from under the little tin hat came the thickest, blackest, air-polluting smoke I had ever seen. It was languorous with its own filth and grease, flowing like oil around the mast and neighboring boats. Dirty, I thought, but not dangerous. I dashed down inside.

General woe. Somewhere Shakespeare says that. I had never understood it before. Every seam and crack was beaming from the wild interior yellow flames. The stove was so hot I backed away from it, trembling hands grabbing for the fire extinguisher. But worst of all—soot. Large thick flakes of oily soot were floating all over the cabin, settling on books and clothes and dishes, soot emerging from every crevice I had not known existed in the stove and pipe. Underfoot, I crunched down on the flakes and powder of my hammering. I drew breath, wept, and poured a drink. This was not what I had in mind when I put my entire savings and income into a boat.

But the danger was past. Neither I nor the boat were on fire. The intake vents were closed, the chimney vents open, and the coal burned slower in control—not my control, but it is a term used often when speaking of fire. True, the stove began to get red-hot, and the cabin temperature soared to 90 degrees, but true also that life was continuing in its stubborn paths. I opened the hatches for air, and settled down with the soot to watch the fire subside.

The next morning I threw the cannel coal overboard and called the Shipmate manufacturer in New Jersey. Pea coal, they said. The one coal I had not yet tried. Will that keep the stove going all night, I asked? The pleasant voice faded into a thoughtful dubiance. Well, with that size of stove, with such a small firebox, it would be very difficult. Of course if you bought a larger stove, the voice brightened, then certainly.

A further flaw in my character is that, when accepting good advice, I only accept those aspects that suit me. This stove was going to stay alight all night. Back to "The People's Coal Company," where my various efforts were being charted with some amusement. I bought 200 pounds of pea coal, and hustled those fat back-breaking sacks down the wobbling docks and into the cockpit.

Throughout the night following the explosion, I had gently meditated on everything that had gone before. The why's and why-not's of various coal sizes and types. Charcoal briquets were larger than pea coal and almost as large as chestnut coal, yet they burned brightly. Cannel coal I had burned in larger lumps and they almost set the boat on fire. Pore spaces were not the problem, but rather the amount of heat required to ignite a mass of coal large enough to sustain itself and in turn ignite its neighbors. I thought of it as a chain reaction wherein each link had to be a certain heat before proceeding to the next. My theory of banking down the fire, good for a large fireplace, simply would not work in a tiny stove.

Now I had a technique that seemed practical. I started the fire with charcoal on a clean grate. When the charcoal was hot and blazing, I added a shovel of coal, sprinkling it over the burning charcoal in one layer. Once the coal was well ignited, I added another layer, and then another, until the firebox was full to the top with burning layers of coal. Only then did I restrict the draught by some 80 percent. In this way the stove's potential was built up to 100 percent, and then, by reducing airflow, the fire was allowed to subside slowly. My log entry for that night read:

Very cold night. Sub zero. *Jabberwock* fixed hard in ice. Changed over to pea coal. Built coal fire on top of charcoal until, layer by layer, it was all red with flame. When firebox was full, closed down stovepipe damper and left a crack open in the vent beneath. FIRE STAYED GOING ALL NIGHT.

That morning the cabin thermometer read 55 degrees, whereas other mornings it had read 35. Inside the stove was a comforting red heart of coal, surrounded by grey ashes and a few unburned coals on the outside. I opened the dampers and threw a few charcoal briquets on the fire, poking the top of the hot coals in the gentlest fashion to ensure that the charcoal would make contact with the hot coals. In about five minutes, a new, refreshed hot flame flared up, the stove warmed, and in about twenty minutes the cabin was up to 70 degrees and water was boiling for coffee and shaving.

I soon discovered that the fire was in a very tender state in the morning. For instance, when I experimented with raking the coals down to get rid of ash, the coals inevitably went out before new coal ignited. It was crucial to rekindle the blaze by the addition of charcoal and only thereafter rake out ashes. Then a fire could be built up that would last for most of the day. I concluded that I was dealing with such a small firebox, only this careful technique could guarantee up to twelve hours of burning and rekindling. It always worked, and I was warm for the remainder of the winter.

There are many advantages to heating with solid-fuel stoves such as a Shipmate. They can be used at sea as well as dockside, and can burn all manner of garbage and bits of driftwood as well as coal. They dry out a boat in a most pleasing way, taking the damp cabin air into the firebox for combustion and expelling it through the stovepipe while radiating heat. An unvented stove, no matter how much heat it produces, cannot help but heat up moist air which is in turn capable of containing even more moisture.

But their greatest advantage, outside of heat, lies in their cooking capacity. I offer it as dogma that food cooked on a cast-iron stove tastes better than the same food prepared on an open-flame stove. Of course, an open flame can supply all the heat needed to provoke the chemistry of cooking. But the warm glow of an iron stove mellows and blends flavors in a very bene-ficial way. It is perfect for making rice, even better for simmering stews. One quickly learns to slide the pan to the hot spot for browning meats or a quick sauté, then sliding the pan back to the gentle heat farthest from the firebox. But always start cooking after a good fire has been prepared and the stove is hot. Nothing is quite so disheartening as a panful of cold onions looking crisp and green alongside a pat of unmelted butter and a furious cook poking viciously at lazy coals.

There is an odd thing about stoves on boats. People tend to lie about them. I have never met a sailor who will admit his stove does not do the trick. Perhaps it is not lying. Perhaps it is an expression of hope, like the memory of an Indian summer. And yet I have spent many a cold evening on other boats when the stove is supposedly lighted and doing well. A peek into the firebox usually reveals a few dark-looking coals smoldering. In general, the problem stems from insufficient heat to get the coals burning, or inadequate draught which can be corrected by lengthening the stovepipe. The longer the pipe, the stronger the draught.

I always used galvanized stovepipe, largely because I didn't get around to having a custom-made pipe made from stainless steel. This would surely be preferable for length of life, safety and easy cleaning, as well as aesthetics. But my galvanized pipe did well enough, even though I had been assured it would rust through within two months. In fact, mine was still going strong after two years of constant use during winter and intermittent use during warm weather.

Many people worry about fire in the stovepipe due to creosote building up. But the risk of this is easily avoided by occasionally making a very hot fire by burning cardboard. This cooks out the creosote before it can build up to a hazardous point. It is the cooler, smoky fire that creates the hazard, for the smoke idles up the chimney, and as it cools it deposits uncombusted solids on the pipe before they can clear the top.

I know only one bad thing about a coal stove, and for that there is an answer. When the stove is out and cold, and a fire is started from paper and kindling, the stovepipe may refuse to draw. The firebox flames, sticks crackle, and you settle back to watch. The effect can be stirring, like a sentimental verson of *The Nut-cracker* on ice. A white smoke comes pouring like molten lead from every crack and crevice, a white falling blanket drifting over the floorboards. It is a beguiling sight, and I have in the past stood watching in foolish intrigue, for that smoke is not easy to clear out of a cabin no matter how well ventilated a boat may be.

What has happened is that the rising heat from the firebox has come smack against the sullen damp cold in the stovepipe, thus forming an inversion layer. The smoke, unable to go up, comes out, all over. The stovepipe must be warmed.

Take a piece of newspaper or the like and set fire to it while removing the hot plate nearest the stovepipe outlet. Stick the burning paper through the opening, directly under the pipe. At first the flame will gutter, but in a moment the sharp heat of the burning paper will prevail and rise, pushing the cold air out. Then is the time to light the stove—after the pipe has been warmed a little.

Watch out on a cloudy day when the air is heavy with moisture drifting off the sea, for the brothers "cold" and "damp" will be huddled in your chimney like an angry thought.

Living on a Boat

LAST NIGHT I dreamed of whales, a pod of them, their
great blackness plunging up the California coast just
beyond where the surf was breaking. It reminded me
of a whale that swam close by my boat in the Pacific
near the Sea of Cortez. It was a white whale.

Knowing that no one would believe I had seen a
white whale, I took a picture of it, and when I showed
this picture to people they suggested that it was not
really white. They said, for instance, that it had been
scarred in some way and that injury, or perhaps poi-
son, accounted for its color.

It was a white whale. And once, coming up on deck
at sunrise far off the coast of Guatemala, I was surrounded by a school of perhaps a hundred dolphins.
They were leaping straight up and clear of the sea,
sluices of water racing off their bodies as they kicked
up and over in the shining morning light. Over and
over, they came up clear, churning the sea into a silver wash until the joy of it seemed one with the radi-
ance of the sun.

This has to do with how I felt on the night I took over my sloop *Jabberwock* and moved on board to live.

There is always a reason for people to take to the sea, especially when their attempt is not merely to reach the far side of an ocean. It is never a casual matter. To decide to live on a boat brings a truly profound change in how one lives and thinks. That was what I wanted, for a loving relationship had ended and I found myself alone in a house I did not wish to be alone in.

My move on board was not a running away to sea in the classic romantic sense. I had done plenty of deep-water cruising at earlier times, learning long ago how to resist the temptation to let life become a line drawn with parallel rulers across the chart to some distant place. No, this was to live on a boat, cruise in good weather when possible, and, since sailing was my hobby anyway, take advantage of all the good watery things possible.

Besides, I had to maintain a job on shore, for that income was needed to purchase and care for a 32-foot sloop. So, while this adventure had dark edges, it seemed sensible enough as a working project. Not that friends necessarily agreed with this. While several of them liked the idea of having access to a large boat for summer sailing, friends less interested in boating thought this move was symptomatic of an impending nervous breakdown. One person asked point-blank, "Is this a way of punishing yourself?"

I think it was not, but it was surely a swift and dramatic shift from one way of life to another, one that

I was ready for, including the dispersal of worldly goods.

A seagoing sloop is a fairly efficient machine, leaving little space for unnecessary baggage. While *Jabberwock* was spacious enough below, there was no space at all in comparison to a house or even a small apartment. Everything that does not matter goes.

I was able to move my library to the dry safety of my office. A good thing, for parting with books is painful. But away went stereos and tape machines and beds and the antique Steinway grand piano, the proceeds from which metamorphosed into anchors, halyards, shackles and insurance. All the unending demands a boat in the water makes.

Clothes were sorted for those items good for sailing or necessary to conduct business. Anything that did not fit into those categories was dumped. The same technique was applied to kitchen equipment, paintings, rugs, all the paraphernalia that life on land collects. It is a little scary perhaps, but it is a wonderful thing to go through the detritus of a life and sift it fine for a new life. It tells where you have been, where you hope to go. Freed of most of the things from a dry world, I turned all attention to what was needed to stay afloat in a wet one. Namely, a good boat.

Buying a boat, the right boat for the right person, is a very tricky thing. It is like getting lovers together in the sense that the chemistry is either there or it is not. You have to fall in love with a boat before you buy it, and love being in the air does not make for clear thinking. It is a subtle and difficult problem.

Who can one believe? The person selling a boat will probably have a moon-sad face as he tells of cruises taken, mishaps survived, and the good qualities of his vessel. The yacht broker, who acts as a matchmaker in these affairs, can say only the most salient and encouraging things, including what a bargain she is on the present market, no matter the price. And you, possessed by the demon of love, are hopeless.

There are three main lines of defense against boat madness of which the first is possibly the most important. That is, the buyer must know what he wants to use the boat for, carefully delineating what qualities she must therefore have.

I wanted a deep-water cruising boat, large enough to make a substantial voyage with two people on board, while her interior had to be spacious and airy enough so that living on board through a long New England winter would not be a claustrophobic experience. At the same time, I wanted a boat small enough to be sailed single-handed, for reliable crews are notoriously difficult to find.

I rejected out of hand a beautiful older wooden boat because she was so deep her cabin was gloomy. Another good boat went the same way because she did not have headroom throughout, and so forth.

There is great interest these days in making plastic boats in the 30-foot category that can sleep six or more people. Tables turn into double beds, bodies are cramped in quarter berths, anything you touch turns magically into a nest for someone. What the designers are going is creating a floating *wagon lit* which is maddeningly uncomfortable and devoid of privacy, even for a weekend cruise. The number of people who can squeeze into these tubs is the selling point, but the design leads to clutter and squabble, while the fact is that a weekend sailor is lucky if he can convince even his wife to go along, let alone enough bodies to fill all the berths. Well-used space is a significant priority, particularly for living on board.

The second line of defense against boat madness is the help of a knowledgeable friend, someone who really knows boats. It is his job to know your objectives so that he can play a hard-nosed devil's advocate. It is so easy for the buyer to gloss over what is not good, how much equipment is worn or on the point of failure. One vaguely notes that the galvanized shrouds are rusting and makes a mental note that stainless steel is preferable anyway. The gennie winches may be too small, or the anchor shaft has a warp in it, and somewhere at the end of the mind lies a fixed and pristine vision of how this new craft will shimmer when you have done all the things you mean to do to her. But these details can mount into thousands of dollars in material and labor. Before you know it, you may have bought a boat within your price range that is in fact out of your price range by the time she is in decent shape. A friend who can make a tough assessment of what is in store by way of replacement and improvement is well worth taking out to dinner.

The final line of defense is a good surveyor. The best surveyor money can buy. It is up to the buyer to find and pay for the surveyor, and, since it is likely that anyone buying a boat will be paying just a little more than he had hoped to pay, it is easy to skimp on surveying expense. But the sins a surveyor can find in the best-looking boat can be both mortal and venal.

When I look back on buying *Jabborwock*, a boat I fell instantly in love with, I rate my behavior in the following way. The selection of the boat was fine, for she served my purposes for cruising and living aboard for two years. My friend who played devil's advocate did well too. I did spend more money than I had imagined, but I was well aware of the areas money was going to be needed in.

My surveyor did me badly, and it pains me to admit that through boat madness this was my fault. By the time the surveyor came to see her, I had already seen her several times and sailed her twice. I had made my decision to buy, provided she passed survey. In short, I was in a state of impassioned euphoria, and I was not keeping proper watch.

I had been in touch with an insurance company from whom I wished coverage. It was they who recommended the surveyor. In other words, the surveyor was working to satisfy the needs of the insurance company as to the risk involved. That was significantly different from my needs which had to do with buying this boat as an investment in addition to her insurability.

When the surveyor came on board, he went over the boat from stem to stern with an impressively

sharp eye. He seemed to miss nothing. He was a big tubby fellow, so I was impressed when he squeezed his gut down into the engine compartment and crawled with much sweating and groaning as far aft as was possible, checking for rust on the hull. He emerged pronouncing her in remarkably good shape.

I asked was he not going to haul her out of the water to check her hull? He replied that he would only do so had he reason to suspect, as he did not, that the hull might not be up to the standards he observed from the inside. He gave her a clean bill of health, and that was that.

It vaguely worried me that she was not hauled. I would have liked to have seen her underwater lines, even though I had been shown pictures of her out of the water. It would have been good to know the condition of the bottom paint, zincs, and the like. But I figured that if the insurance company was pleased enough to issue a policy, that should be sound enough judgment for me. What I had not considered was that the company could care less whether she sank or swam. They wanted only to ascertain that she was an insurable risk.

For them, it was a matter of statistics. They cared, for instance, that her batteries were placed in an acid-proof box, for, in the event of a capsize, acid might spill with scalding results. They wanted my through-hull fittings replaced for no reason except that they were original and Dutch. While I had no desire to see a fitting fail, why risk putting in new fittings in a steel

hull when the old ones are clearly good? The likelihood of electrolysis from uniting dissimilar metals is
a corrosive danger.

Just as they were unconcerned about checking her
bottom, they were equally unconcerned about my
sailing abilities, allowing me to sail from Maine to
Florida amidst all possible peril. Real risk was not of
concern. *Jabberwock* was insurable because she fit
their requirements in terms of their statistics.

I cannot blame them. It was just that I did not know
enough about such things at the time. I assumed that
our interests were mutual when they were not. I was
in love with the boat and was happy to hear what I
wanted to hear. The error in this became clear the
following season when I hauled for repainting.

The foot of her keel had corroded badly at some
point in the past. The cunning previous owner had
been hard at work patching it poorly with fiberglass.
Furthermore, this leaky mess had allowed water to
seep in and around the ballast so that much of the
keel was in a weakened state. Had she been properly
surveyed, this patching with fiberglass would have
been readily apparent. Under no circumstance would
I then have bought her. It was a lesson hard learned.

But it also points, this slow seeping underwater, to
what all boat owners live with. The opposite of floating is sinking, and no matter how efficiently a boat
has been surveyed, or how carefully she is kept up,
every boat owner must enjoy his tenure on board in
the company of that dark mate who pulls her down.
To live half in air and half in water is what floating is

about. What buoys one up is a sinking feeling, something to be resisted. Everything has its price.

So the boat was bought, and what lingered below lay waiting. The first job was to get to know her. Boats, like people, look simple enough from a distance, but they are just as complicated in their idiosyncrasies. Was the tiny drip from the head a leak that required fixing, or was this the way the head liked to work best? Why was the cooling system for the engine putting out so little water? Why was the mast leaning slightly to port? Did the depth finder tell the truth?

The shrouds were adjusted, a pound of river weed removed from the engine, the head was left alone, and the like. Heads are curious things. They lead a life of their own. When people gather for drinks on a particular boat, they will inevitably trot off down the dock to their own boat and use their own head rather than be found feckless before the machinations of a strange one.

In short, within the first few hours of my moving on board, I was already involved with putting things awry to aright. This particular process has probably more to do with living on a boat than any other. It is nonending. Anyone who wants to live aboard had better enjoy this continual fixing and replacing and jury-rigging, as well as the anticipated general maintenance. It can be taxing and wearisome, but it is a great teacher.

Because assistance is so often hard to come by, and comes at a high price, one learns to look at problems with more care than on land. You learn to deal with things. An engine that lapses into silence after running satisfactorily may well have no fuel or a blocked fuel line.

Since this sort of problem almost never arises at the dock, but more likely in a narrow channel when you are going upstream, or when you are being blown onto a lee shore and depending on the engine to get you out of trouble, you cope. Throw the anchor overboard, or tie up to a buoy, and fix it. It is amazing what even an amateur mechanic can accomplish by considering what the problem may be, looking at how the machine works, taking things to pieces and putting them back together again. With decent tools on board, remarkably little know-how, and the pressing encouragement of danger, things get fixed. It is an enormously rewarding experience.

Boats are such consoling places to sleep. They are, I suppose, the ultimate water beds. The soft liveliness of their forgiving motion, even in still water, is soothing. They sway to a step, a quality one is quickly reminded of when they are up on land. There they feel stiff and unloving, in need of water.

But no matter how beguiling boats are to sleep on, there are other considerations. Those might be called "little things in the night." The boat is safely stowed and anchored, or docked at a secure float. It is a good feeling to know the boat is in no danger when you drop off to sleep. As sleep lingers in her smooth, dreamy ways, something comes knocking. Perhaps there is a wind change, or perhaps the tide drops lower than charts and tables suggest so that the keel

touches bottom. Maybe a wash from a distant boat coming home late suddenly shakes. Always something, and always come those little noises.

You wake, like an animal, eyes wide, breath held even before the brain is conscious. What one really hears is vulnerability. For all the strength and design a seagoing boat may have, it is subject to happenstance that may wreck it in an instant. Why are the blocks creaking when no line is running through them? Why is the hull suddenly grinding against the fenders? What do those hollow-sounding bubbles running up the hull signify? What made the rudder bonk on its pinions just then? Are you adrift?

These starts of paranoia are usually quickly answered. Indeed the wind has changed. Indeed the lines are straining. A boat has gone by, sharing its unexpected wake with you. Generally all will be well. It is just the boat responding, adjusting to her environment. For the most part, she will look after you better than you can look after her.

But the unexpected does happen. It can and will happen, which is why we wake up, like animals, alert to the needs of self-preservation. In Saint Thomas one night, I was fast asleep and woke with the feeling that the boat had capsized. I leaped up and ran on deck to see a full-sized ship that had previously been moored a hundred yards away trying to turn her whole length in that tiny space. She was a freighter just disgorged of her cargo so that she rode high in the water, her enormous prop beating up and clear of the water as she tried to maneuver through a semicircle. Her bow was up close to the pier she was leaving, and her stern, with its scything blades swiping and cutting, was swinging right at us.

As she came at us, standing fifty feet above, her crew was leaning over the after rail staring in glee and wonder at our predicament. The surge of water that her props set up in her effort to turn swept around us, a wave of running water sucking between the dock and the hull. Lines were popping, and as we put new ones on, the hull was lifted up and dashed against the dock. We were held off the dock by a breast line, and, as the fierce windmill of a prop came down on us, threatening to cleave the hull, it sliced the breast line and half of the hull landed on the dock before sliding back with a smash into the water.

We were both terrified and infuriated. Outside of damage to line and paint no harm was done. But an infuriated letter to the owners of the ship was not responded to. Our only satisfaction was a visit the next day from the local pilot. He had a hangover, or so his trembling seemed to indicate. He told us that he and the captain of the ship had made a drunken bet, he betting that he could turn the ship in that reach of water, the captain betting that he could not. I am entirely unclear as to who won the bet. I know we did not.

As a general rule, I switch off the batteries when not in use, and certainly when I am not on board. Like all general rules, this one sometimes got broken. At a time when I had a lot of work to do in the city, I stayed there temporarily with friends, leaving *Jabberwock* safely alone at her slip.

It happened that I got lonely for her, so I decided to drop by one day and have lunch on board to say hello. As I was sitting in the main cabin a spume of smoke suddenly pushed out of the woodwork where the wires to the starboard running lights pushed through. I looked at it in utter disbelief for a moment. Then a splutter of sparks had me on my feet and running to the battery switch which I had inadvertently left on.

It turned out that general wear and tear, plus corrosion, had dilapidated the wires until, at that instant, they shorted out. Had I not by chance been on board, she would in all likelihood have burned to the water's brim. It was a horrifying thought, and thereafter I was absolutely strict about turning all electrics off.

It was this sort of problem that made living on board over long periods of time a strain for me. Keeping a good-sized vessel in repair and sailing shape is possibly a half-time job or more, especially if you do all of the work yourself. Since I had a full-time job on land for the first year of residence, and during the second I was on board writing full-time, I found myself beginning to rely more and more on shipyards to do work for me professionally.

This was a woeful expense. I kept thinking that when I got the boat to a certain level, she could be maintained with minimal expenditure. But that never quite seemed to happen. Furthermore, when there was nothing that urgently needed care, I was incapable of not making improvements. Installing a new water filter for the cooling system, for instance, or fitting new blocks and tracks on the deck to give the gennie a better set.

I had expected her old Hercules gas engine to give out the year I bought her; for it was saltwater cooled and ten years old—just about the length of time one can hope to keep a saltwater engine going. And it did give out, though for other, oily reasons.

I planned to replace it with a Volva Penta diesel engine which is a fine piece of machinery and has the wonderful advantage of getting gasoline off the boat. Gasoline is very dangerous, its fumes, when they escape, building in the bilges until they form an explosive mix. At that point, the very word "spark" can set it off with disastrous results. Several boats blow up every year on Narragansett Bay alone from gasoline fumes.

The new engine was a dream. But to mount it required the installation of new engine mounts, and, because diesel fuel does not live happily in galvanized tanks, my old tanks had to be replaced with steel ones. A new exhaust system was also needed to get the right flow of water from the cooling system, so, all in all, replacing the engine was twice as difficult and twice as expensive as I had estimated. I can multiply, but it is often frightening.

The new engine had the problems of all new toys. Bits and pieces fell off from vibrations, and one particular problem took a long time to solve. The engine went like a bomb for an hour and then conked out. By bleeding air from the bleeding screws, and a lot of air bubbled up, the engine would restart. But where was the air coming from? Air in diesel fuel is as sure a way of stopping the engine as sugar mixed into a gasoline engine. It took several days of fiddling to discover that the fuel tap shutoff, one designed for gasoline, allowed a wisp of air to sneak into the diesel fuel as it flowed by. When air bubbles collected in the fuel injectors, the engine failed. Once that was replaced, all was well.

But all was not well with the engine, even though it was now running well and pushing the boat mightily. To dock *Jabberwock,* she had to be brought up a river that flowed at perhaps three knots. This meant that a good deal of power was required to push her upriver through the current before moving into the stiller water of the turning basin where the docks were. Once in quiet water, I had to make a 180-degree turn into her slip with the way off her.

I came up the river, pushing ahead like mad, and when I pulled her out of gear in the still water to put her in reverse, the gears were jammed. I wanted to sidle forward into the slip, but the gears would not disengage. She seemed to be going at ten knots as we made a fast circle towards the dock. There was nothing for it but to turn off the engine and make a spectacular and speedy attack at the dock, narrowly swiping by the sterns of moored boats, and hitting the slip so that she rode up over it for a few feet with the usual loss of some paint.

It was not until I inspected the engine oil that the explanation came. The gears were integral with the oil lubricating system. By foul chance, water had infiltrated the oil so that it turned milky white with an accompanying loss of viscosity. The gears had lost their heft.

The engine had to be removed and x-rayed. This showed that a pinhole fracture in the engine head had allowed cooling water into the lubricating system. Luckily enough the guarantee covered such a mishap. But when the engine was replaced, the gears had frozen into the forward position because salt water had fouled them into their jammed position. That, in turn, meant that the transmission had to be removed and cleaned. After that, all was fine. But this is what one puts up with, even when spending ready money.

Perhaps people who live in houseboats, say in Sausalito near San Francisco, or in Florida, where houseboating has become as fashionable as buying condominiums, have it easier. Their boats are made to float without the need to sail. They are docked apartments that do not need to have the ability to go to sea. Many of them manage gardens floating off the stern on rafts, and they are replete with all manner of airconditioners and central heating. But even though they are lame ducks as boats, I cannot imagine that they get off scot-free when it comes to the nature of the corrosive environment in which they sit.

One pays a price for living on a boat. It is two-fold. One is money, the second is time. They are interchangeable depending on your skills, but pay you will, depending on your talents.

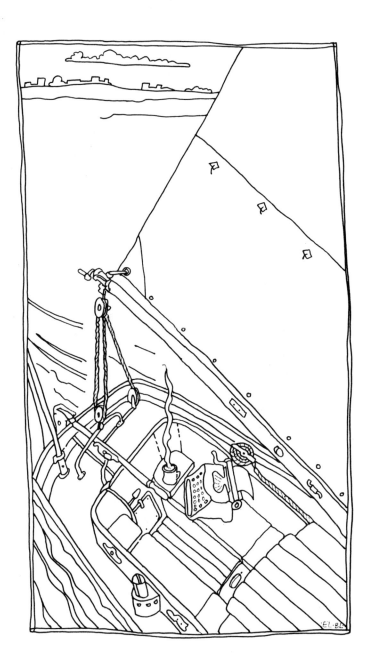

It was such harangue that discouraged me from living on board for a third year. I began to discover that maintaining the boat in good order made other work impossible. Time and money built up to a point where the joy of living on board was outweighed by needs of survival and work.

The type of incident and experience I point to is not unique. It is simply my own. I know many people who have lived on boats, and who still do. They all have the same story. Only the details are different. All of us loved our boats, boats in general, and all of us deeply cared for the way of life that living on a boat implied. We were happy to spend the time and money in pursuit of it.

But one by one, we found that keeping a boat up took too much time from careers. One by one, we discovered that to run off to New York and design a show, or write a new book, or even visit friends in other places, set such burdens that the joy began to be tarnished. Sailing was no less wonderful, and the peace of floating at anchor on an evening still held its delicate delights. But the battle to keep things in order, to maintain a seagoing boat, to not let her sink from invidious corrosion or accident which is the birthright of floating things, became wearisome.

What never got wearisome was the actual living aboard. Yes, showers were few, ice was a problem, laundry was a bore. But if one were to subtract continual maintenance, the galloping expenses and the various anxieties, then having a home on a boat was snugly perfect. Once I gave up my city job and was writing full-time on board, able to keep the boat wherever I chose, that was as close to ideal as I know.

During my last months on *Jabberwock* she was in very good shape indeed. Her hull was painted kitti-wake blue, topsides were oyster white. The teak rails and mahogany doors and hatches were lustrous with varnish. She looked very shipshape. Her aft pulpit was hung with spare lines and rope fenders. Gerry cans for extra fuel and water were lashed there too. Anchors and rodes were stowed flat on the foredeck. The shrouds were wound with baggy-wrinkle, and a simple awning stretched from the twin backstays to the shrouds. She looked workmanlike, a boat that went places.

Down below was home. The galley and chart areas were spacious and functional. Forward, the main cabin contained a sizable library, a table with space near the hull to store my typewriter, and a deacon's bench good for keeping everything from tax returns to manuscripts, passports and checkbooks. The cushions were newly upholstered, and the wood glistened in the glint of the kerosene lamps. The coal stove with its chimney rising through the deck puffed out heat when needed. A big copper kettle simmered on the hot plates.

Forward of the enclosed head and hanging locker were two long, comfortable V-berths. For a touch of color and decadence, the cabin sole was scattered with Persian rugs. They looked very good and took well to salt water.

It was a strange and wonderful thing to sail into a

new port, a new place to explore and investigate, with all the strangeness of new places in the air. Then to come back to the rich familiarity of home, a home that contained all the things I required to go on with work and the business of daily living. It was lovingly secure.

I would like to end it there, walking back through a strange port on a foggy evening, hopping into the dinghy at a pier and rowing out to the twinkling anchor light. To go on board, to the warmth and light and comfort of the good things that boats can offer. To check the anchor, and close the hatches, and to snuggle down for a night's sleep.

But that is not how it ended. That is not how things end. For close to the end of my natural tenure on board, I was offered a lot of money for *Jabberwock*, much more than she was worth. All boats are for sale. It is only a question of the price. So I began to think, and I thought, soon after, that I had done this living on board long enough. I did put her up for sale, at a price that allowed me to get out the money I had put into her.

She failed survey, because of her keel. So I sold her for a song to a young man who loved her at a glance. He was a welder and shipwright. He planned to make her whole in ways that I could not. I was glad he loved her, saw what a ship she was. But when he trucked her away, I could not look.

Concrete Ghosts

To BUILD A BOAT and sail into the azure seas. It is an alluring fantasy that seizes many a good heart, and many a good heart is broken by the tyrannical god who presides over human folly.

About a decade ago, the concept of building concrete boats hit the market, and the market was ripe for it. The Kennedys had managed to get a surprising number of people away from television sets and out into the open air to jog and camp and hike. The do-it-yourself syndrome was on an upswing. Many Americans were more and more interested in breaking away from city routines and the passivity of pre-packaged amusement.

The concrete boat people, whether by accident or design, packaged their product in such a way as to take advantage, fairly gross advantage, of this new market. The attack was two-fold. Advertising suggested that a 54-foot concrete ketch could be built for as little as 15,000 dollars and that such a boat could be built by amateurs possessing only minimal skills.

On the surface of it, it appeared that anyone who so desired could have the boat of his dreams for a song and a year or so of part-time labor. This is not the case.

Nevertheless, good hearts were seized. Plans began to sell like hotcakes. Soon the landscape of America was dotted with half-finished hulls, upturned behemoths, abandoned and lost on the land just as surely as their builders' dreams of having a fine vessel for little money were lost in the night. Some maudlin-looking boats, improperly plastered and finished, made it into the water, and ferro-cement began to get a bad name.

That was a pity. While concrete hulls have not been tested for seaworthiness to the same extent as hulls of other materials such as plastic, there is much to indicate that ferro-cement hulls are very good indeed.

The concrete boat is constructed by interweaving steel rods to the shape of the hull. This is in turn rolled with wire mesh which is employed to hold the concrete skin that makes the boat watertight. Done properly, the hull is both very strong and flexible. Damage usually remains localized in what is known as an egg-shell fracture, and this allows for relatively simple jury repair with underwater epoxy. Like the plastic hull, the concrete hull provides considerably more interior space than a wooden hull, while a good finish can look as bright and shipshape as one could wish.

Unfortunately, what haunts our dreams and what, in fact, sails the seas are not the same things, as Plato pointed out long ago. I have known personally three people who were seized by the idea of building in concrete, and the first two names will be withheld to protect the guilty.

Mr. X was a designer with considerable mechanical abilities. He went into the concrete business with all the enthusiasm of a Catholic convert, insisting that concrete boats were the boats of the future, and piling his small apartment with rolls of chicken wire, welding equipment and the like. Outside, in a low swamp near a tidal river, his wooden mold arched skyward. I remember him sitting astraddle the keel, the evening growing cold and dark, while the flare and spark of his welding torch burned and crackled. Several months of steady work were stopped by winter, and the spring attack carried less impetus than formerly. The hope was frequently expressed that by the following month the chicken wire would go on, and plans were made for a plastering party. There were many following months, and as Mr. X welded and watched boats afloat drift down the river, he thought to buy a boat, in part financed by the sale of his half-completed hull.

After several weeks of advertising, the rolls of chicken wire were purchased by a chicken farmer. The hull still lies upside down in the swamp where it looks like a rusting beached whale.

Mr. Y was a librarian with a dogged attitude about getting things done. Unfortunately he had the notion that when the hull was finished it was time to go to sea. When the hull was crudely done, so was his money. It is generally accepted that the cost of a hull is about 15 percent of the cost of the finished boat. So Mr. Y, under pressure to move to New York for professional reasons, began to think of rigging his ketch as a junk, using telephone poles for masts.

He launched his boat near Chicago and set off, ill-equipped and worse advised, across the Great Lakes under power alone. One of those vicious lake storms got him. His engine failed, as did his electrics. He attempted to anchor with an inadequate line which soon parted, and the boat was swept aground. His wife fell down the companionway where there were no stairs and broke her arm. After some time, the Coast Guard rescued them, mercifully enough. When last heard of, the still incomplete boat was abandoned, moored in a quiet backwater with a For Sale sign stuck on her.

Kurt Hammer is the third person I know to have attempted the arduous task of building a concrete boat. He and his family have worked unceasingly for the past seven years on the project. The result is the 46-foot schooner, *Peer Gynt,* a magnificent vessel, presently moored in Channel Islands Marina in California. Kurt has just completed her wooden masts which will be stepped within a couple of weeks. It is a great success story. But there was a price.

Seven years ago, I happened to be visiting Kurt and Marianne at their home in Camarillo, California. Home for them has been many places since they left

WIRE

·EL·BL·

Norway, and their three children have passports
from three different countries. I had a feeling of dismay on learning that plans for a concrete boat were
underway. But I tried to mask this, tried not to think
of the other projects I had seen stagger to a disap-
pointing and expensive halt.

Kurt showed me a wooden pram sailing dinghy he
had built by way of an aperitif. In the garage was a
growing collection of welding equipment, tools and
the ubiquitous chicken wire. The study walls were
covered in blueprints and sketches with intricate calculations, for Kurt, while using the basic Samson
Marine Design "C-Deuce" ketch plan, was making
considerable changes which included rigging the boat
as a staysail schooner. This did not surprise me, for
Kurt is a highly skilled engineer, adept at design, and
well used to thinking projects through from scratch.

Some six months had been spent on plans and
gathering information on the project. A library,
about 300 dollars worth of books, had been studied.
The underwater profile was altered to balance the
rigging change, and the long flat keel of the original
had been ameliorated. In an attempt to improve
steering, the deadwood was whittled down, feathered
almost to a sharp edge to allow a better flow of water
into the prop, and, in addition, the rudder was air-
foiled.

The theory of this intrigued me. I am well accustomed to expect sluggish steering in a large sailboat,
and more likely no steering at all in reverse. But Kurt
was correct, for, when *Peer Gynt* was launched, she

turned on a dime, and was equally controllable in reverse.

The commitment and knowledge Kurt was bringing to bear on his plans were impressive. But still my dismay kept jiggling, for the project as he outlined it seemed to swell larger and larger. It would involve the entire family's efforts, finances, and time over at least a three-year period, and after that there was the plan of a world cruise ending up, naturally enough, in Norwegian waters.

It was not until we returned to the living room that my dismay was assuaged—for sitting on the floor were Kurt's teenage daughters, Annelin and Yvette. In front of them was a cardboard box filled with wooden cleats, handsomely carved and finished. The girls had made them. Their first step. I looked at the cleats on the floor, and thought of the plans on the study walls. All that was needed was to fill in the gap. "I think you're going to make it," I said to Kurt. There wasn't a trace of gloom in his twinkling blue eyes.

The years wandered on, and about once a year I happened to be in their part of California, stopping by for a visit and an appreciative look at work accomplished. In place of chicken wire was six layers of galvanized square welded mesh which was harder to work with, but stronger. The pastering was completed, and after that, the joke, aimlessly repeated, became tiresome—When will she be in the water? The answer was always a fair calculation that one more year would do it.

What began as a project aimed at changing a way of life, had become a way of life in itself. Month after month, the regular business of life was taken care of, and then the life of the boat took over. Every evening, each weekend and holiday, the work went on with almost no respite. I don't know how he managed the patience, the stamina, the fortitude to keep going— except that he told me in his wry and ironic way, "You do one thing and then you do another." Occasionally I have managed that myself.

But the time did come. The hull was sanded smooth and sealed, the engine, tanks and lines were installed, the galley was in, and most of the interior was roughed out. I didn't see her then, on the exultant day when the wall at the foot of the garden was broken down and a flatbed truck took the glistening dream of a boat to the marina. The local newspapers covered the event, and Marianne did the honors of smashing a bottle of champagne over her bow before she dipped, in perfect balance, into the water.

It is a silly detail, but worth recording—Kurt had scored the champagne bottle with a glass cutter to insure that it would shatter in the appropriate fashion. That is the level of care and forethought that went into every aspect of his work.

The launching came almost seven years after the project began. The sustained effort to reach this particular point had been so great that an understandable lassitude seemed to creep into the family now that the major push was over. Kurt and his son Kurt Jr. visited relatives in Norway. Annelin was working on

an oil rig in the North Sea. It was Marianne and
Yvette who met me on the dock to let me see *Peer Gynt*
afloat. It was as though their accustomed buoyancy
was lodged in the ship now. One way of life had
ended, and the sea faring one to come seemed like
another impossible project. At the same time, one
sensed in them a pride and an amazement that so
much had been accomplished so well. But the price
was getting high. It was clear that building a concrete
boat was no casual matter.

Over the years, I had gathered enough information
to have a general sense of what such a project
entailed, but I was anxious to hear from Kurt directly
his reflections on the specifics. So when the family
reassembled, I joined them for a meal, and in the best
Conradian tradition of speaking about boats, we sat
around the table and "passed the bottle."

Kurt immediately allowed that were he to do it over
again he would buy a well-made plastic hull, and start
from there. There was no loss of faith on his part for
concrete as hull material, but the working of it he
described as "a hard thankless grind." Steel and concrete lacked all aesthetic appeal for him, and, apart
from the pleasure of seeing the hull take on its final
shape when the wire mesh was put on, the two years
and 3000 hours of labor were very short on joy.

Many people building these boats regard the vital
addition of the plaster an occasion for a party where
they gather as many friends together as they can mus-
ter to sling mud. The element of a grape-crushing
festival has its appeal, but the results are likely to be

dangerous, for the key in plastering is to get it on so as to avoid dry spots which would later crumble out. The three-quarter-inch thickness of the hull must be maintained as evenly as possible.

Kurt hired professional plasterers, seven of them, who had done some 130 boats previously, and these men were aided by 23 amateurs. The work was done in one long day after which the curing process began. Curing concrete is an axious making business, for it must cure slowly, being continually hosed down with water to ensure cracks do not develop as can happen with quick drying.

While Kurt was at work, Marianne crawled about inside the cavernous, dank hull faithfully keeping it damp for thirty days. I think she was allowed out occasionally, but her memory of this time still makes her shudder. And it was about this time that Kurt's concerns began to poke through in dreams. In one of his dreams, the concrete flowed like treacle from the metal and hung as great udders on either side of the keel. In another, all of the concrete washed away, and Marianne, who is lithe and small, had moved the vast bulk of the hull which occupied the entire garden and shrunk it to a miniature toy boat in order to water the grass. Meanwhile, in daylight, they both searched for dry spots feeling the terror with which a victim of bubonic plague might scan his body for the first rupture on the skin.

But the plasterers had done a fine job. The hull cured without mishap, and anxieties were eased by an extensive and thorough survey done by professional marine surveyors. The same team surveyed the boat again before she was launched, and provided an excellent documentation of every aspect of the boat. This is invaluable information to have when buying insurance and in the event the boat should ever be sold.

Thus far, the expense of producing the bare hull was 3,353 dollars, and that was in 1974. Kurt allows that the product, if well made, is a beautiful one, easy in matters of upkeep and repairs. But while the building in concrete requires less skill than similar work in wood or even plastic, it does involve great care, and it is not cheap.

By the time *Peer Gynt* was launched, the Hammers had invested 42,000 dollars in her. And it should be said that, while all the materials and equipment put on board were of high grade, Kurt shopped with great care to get the best possible bargains through cooperatives, buying in bulk, and the like. It is likely that a well-found concrete boat of this size cannot be made for less. It should be noted that, in this instance, the hull cost proved to be 8 percent of the finished boat cost.

On the face of it, 42,000 dollars for a handsome deep-water schooner sounds cheap enough. But that price contains no allowance for labor. Kurt's carefully maintained records indicate that he alone put in 9,750 hours of work over the seven-year building period. Were a meager allowance of 10 dollars an hour for his highly skilled labor introduced, the cost of the vessel becomes 139,500 dollars. That is probably close to the going market price of any well-built schooner of that size. Not cheap indeed!

But, at least, the hull was formed and set; the most barren work from an aesthetic stand point was finished. Meanwhile, there was an enormous gain, for something that looked very like a boat now occupied the garden, its bow protruding over the wall.

It became a landmark, this huge gray duck poking its bill into a perfectly ordinary street, surrounded by indistinguishable houses in a development. The neighbors gawked in a neighborly way, and the Hammers, who for so long had belonged both to several countries and to nowhere, became one with their ark. It was, at any rate, their focus.

The children went to school, except that some of them were no longer children, and after college the two girls traveled about the world. The work went on; one project completed, another one began. But the work was much more pleasing now. Kurt rethought and designed hundreds of improvements in regard to tanks, plumbing, the use of space. A diesel engine of only 22 horsepower was installed with a 24-inch feathering prop. Kurt considers most sailboats are overpowered and underpropped. I don't know and wait to see how she pushes ahead into wind with a stiff chop. But since I have observed him to be correct on his other estimates, I choose not to hazard a guess on the sufficiency of the power source.

I did become concerned about the size of the cockpit which is a central type that allows for a large double-berth cabin aft. Such a cabin is a blessed thing when cruising, for, no matter how loving shipmates are, love blooms anew after not seeing someone for twelve hours. The original cockpit was very large indeed, a space pleasant for day-sailing, but poor, in my experience, for cruising. It is hard for the helmsman to gain good purchase in a large cockpit in rough weather, and it is usually harder to reach from the wheel for sheets, instruments, or simply to grab a cup of soup being passed up the companionway. But the greatest disadvantage of too large a cockpit is the weight of water it can hold after a sea breaks into it. That can be crippling, and even self-bailing cockpits take considerable time to empty. I had urged Kurt to make his cockpit much smaller, which he did, and gained valuable space below as a result. But sitting in it, I had a slightly confined feeling, for although it sits four people readily, it is deep enough and short enough to make me question my idea.

In any event, the work went on for almost five years after the hull was cured. Kurt proved himself adept in all the skills of the shipwright's trade. The interior was finished in mahogany, cap rails and hatches were made from teak. The masts were made from spruce, and even the metal fittings for the rigging were redesigned and made by hand. Kurt had planned to employ deadeyes and lanyards to fasten the shrouds, but comparative pricing and possible efficiency persuaded him to use turnbuckles.

Through all of this, Marianne worked alongside, as did the three children when they were home from school or home from Europe. I do not know how they did it. The vast scope and longevity of the project would have driven me away in frustration. But they stuck it out. And if there were occasions for anger and irony, it seemed to me that this was a ship of ships, one that had needfully appeared at a particular time in the lives of these particular people.

There had been decades of wandering since Kurt and Marianne first left Norway. Now they have built a boat in which to wander home, and they called it after Peter Gynt who was himself a wanderer from Norway in search of his soul through travel and adventure. I do not mention this to be fanciful, but to point out that when people undertake great tasks, it is always for profound reasons. These reasons often transcend immediate considerations through which the race sustains itself. To be open to such things, to dare and ride with them, can give one's life the stirring reverberations more often recorded in works of art than experienced in the daily business of a more settled life.

Kurt is correct when he says, "The joy of boating is its unpredictability. Life as tepid soup is boring—and boredom is rarely something the sea allows." But then the question is, How much unpredictable joy can any of us bear?

"Fear," Kurt says, by way of a reply, "is the great motivator of our lives." And I suppose these concepts are aspects of the next project the Hammers will investigate.

I asked Kurt to summarize what the building experience had meant to him. He spoke very thoughtfully, saying that it had improved his life in many ways. It had developed in him a sense of confidence and self-reliance, for every skill he had ever picked up, including bits and pieces of craft he had learned in farming as a child, had been put to use. As to the work involved in building a concrete boat, he says, "It is a long, long, long, hard, hard, hard commitment."

We sat around the table, drinking Scotch. We had stopped discussing the technicalities of building boats. There was something in the air that we were all aware of, but that no one seemed quite ready to express. We had spent a loving time together. Somewhere, the ghost of a great white schooner drifted.

Going through the Panama Canal

IT IS A CALM EXCITEMENT. That in itself is surprising, but the business of the canal is so carefully articulated in its workings and organization that high drama and accident are adroitly avoided.

All the same, it is a stirring place. Shipping from one half of the globe converges from Atlantic waters, piling up off the port of Cristobal where each ship lies at anchor waiting in turn to squeeze through the narrow channel into the vast flood of the Pacific. On the southern, Pacific, end, ships from the Orient wait off Balboa to slip one by one into the warm Caribbean and off to the old world.

It is a place as international as the United Nations.

Russian warships sidle by Libyan freighters. The Red Duster of Britain flutters near the French Tricolor. It is here that one can glimpse the international commerce of the seas that Joseph Conrad knew so well. Sterns are marked with the names of the great ports of registry—Amsterdam, Bergen, London. The list conjures the entire globe into this tiny waterway.

The Panama Canal is an awesome feat of engineering, and simple enough in its principles. But what defeated, or almost defeated, both the French who first attempted a canal, and the Americans who finally succeeded, was disease. Panama's hot and humid tropical climate was perfect for the mosquito to flourish in and the yellow fever which is transmitted by its bite claimed the lives of hundreds of workers. Yellow fever is a horrible disease that causes degeneration of the cells in the liver, spleen, kidney and heart. Death results in some 60 percent of severe cases.

Colonel Walter Reed, working in Cuba after the Spanish-American war, was the first person to make the connection between mosquitoes and yellow fever. This information was brought to Panama by Colonel William C. Gorgas of the United States Medical Corps. He eradicated the breeding grounds of the mosquito, screened windows, and piped fresh, clean water into the cities. By 1905, yellow fever had disappeared from the area, and the engineering proceeded safely.

The Isthmus of Panama is fifty miles across and mountainous. Unlike the Suez Canal which is a sea-level ditch connecting the Red Sea with the Mediterranean, the Panama Canal had to be constructed so as to take ships over the hills. To do this, a system of locks was employed to raise a vessel some 85 feet above sea level. At that height, a man-made lake was created by damming the turbulent Chagres River, and this lake is large enough to account for the major portion of the passage from coast to coast. On the far side of the lake, another system of locks lowers the ship to sea level again.

The man-made Gatun Lake is crucial to the operation of the locks, for it supplies the water which floods the locks by gravity flow, all the locks being at lake level or below. When a ship is enclosed in one of the locks, some 26-million gallons of water are required to elevate it approximately 28 feet. Luckily, water in Panama is a bountiful resource. The Pacific Ocean side of the Isthmus receives 68 inches of rain annually, while the Atlantic side receives 130 inches. Enough water is retained by the dams to secure the operation of the canal during the few dry months of the year.

About 37 ships pass through the canal every day. Each ship is guided by a pilot whose authority while he is on board supersedes that of the captain. This is the only instance in the seagoing world where the captain waves his authority to a pilot, and the reason for it becomes clear when the difficulties of navigating the twisting eight-mile Gallaird Cut are observed, while the trick of sliding a ship into one of the locks has the problematic appearance of getting a ship into a bottle.

There were three of us on board the ketch *August Moon,* moving westward through the Caribbean toward the canal. We had been in unpleasant weather, a force-8 gale, for three days, and had been blown off course towards Jamaica more than we wanted. When the storm system moved out, there was a flat calm, so there was nothing for it but to turn on the big diesel and bang away for the final day and night before landfall.

The night was one of those dark nights so black ·and hot and cloying, it was like being smothered in velvet. The compass had to be relied on for any sense of direction, and, on watch, I experienced a claustrophobic sense of being utterly lost, as though a childish game of blind man's bluff had gone on too long at my expense. Just before the watch changed, there was a dry lightning storm. Jagged bolts of electricity that looked as though they had been sketched by a comic-book artist tore the sky, some of them so close to us, I thought I could see them boil into the water.

At the same time, converging as we were on the canal, we found ourselves on a collision course with half a dozen other vessels. It always amazes me that by seemingly impossible odds, when two vessels occupy the same square mile of water, they always seem to manage a collison course. I learned long ago that those who keep watch on seagoing freighters are very sleepy fellows indeed.

It is good not to dwell on such things on a dark night, and I crawled into a damp berth, trying not to think of collison or the effectiveness of the mast as a lightning conductor. When I awoke, we were anchoring off Cristobal.

When the immigration officials came on board, they were very civilized, provided us with a huge bug bomb spray, and gave one of the crew a smallpox vaccination on the spot. But then they muddled us with so much paperwork, no sarcastic metaphor could do it justice. The United States government is like that, worse than any other I have encountered. The only thing to do is be docile and subservient, for complaint may bring forth yet another form and six copies.

After that, they disputed the stated length of *August Moon*. This was no small thing, for they claimed her overall length was some three feet shorter. It is all right to have the size of your boat overestimated, but the reverse is downright insulting. Whereupon they produced a tape measure and proved themselves correct. Things are smartly done in Panama, but we had the slender advantage of having to pay less for our passage through the canal.

We were allowed to dock at the yacht club where we got a prime berth at a floating dock not twenty feet from the bar and restaurant. Yacht clubs are often very happy places to put into when cruising. Provided you belong to a recognized club yourself, most clubs will offer visitors their guest dock and permit the use of facilities for a limited stay. It is more pleasant than being tied up at a strange commercial dock, and safer too. It is also surprisingly easy to strike up friendships with people interested in sailing, and we were often entertained in private homes or taken on tours of the area we happened to be passing through. Meanwhile, the natives get to hear the stories that every cruising sailor accrues, while they enjoy being invited aboard a yacht that is merely pausing in the midst of a long voyage.

For now, it was very good to sit over a hot meal and admire the boat floating safely beyond the restaurant window, especially after a tiring week at sea. We were always tired when we got to port. Keeping watch around the clock takes its toll. The cook took three-hour watches, while the other two had four-hour stints. That meant four hours at the helm followed by seven hours off.

On paper, the seven-hour period seems adequate for rest. But that is not the case. Sail changes are frequently necessary, and that requires all hands on deck, while there is the continual need for sewing sails, repairing gear, pumping bilges, navigation, eating and cleaning up. In effect, the seven-hour period rarely allows for even four hours of uninterrupted sleep, so fatigue becomes a major factor on any voyage that lasts longer than three days. In general, we found ourselves at sea for about seven days at a time, and once the boat was safely secured in port and a decent meal eaten, we slept around the clock.

We lay in Cristobal for three days while making arrangements to pass through the canal. You cannot just go at the canal, as through a toll plaza on a turnpike. Each ship must be admeasured, cargo and destination recorded. The canal fee may amount to thousands of dollars for a large ship, while the cruising yacht pays but a nominal sum. In our case, the fee could not even have covered the pilot's salary for the day. Then we had to wait our turn.

Friends we made at the yacht club took us out to explore Cristobal and Colon. With so much shipping passing through the canal, the stores are crammed with exotic goods, and prices seemed very low in contrast to those in the United States. Indeed, contrast is everywhere.

The Canal Zone is handsomely maintained. Red roofs, freshly painted walls, spacious and well-tended lawns suggest an easy life of wealth and order. But immediately beyond the Zone was a display of poverty I had only read of before. Many of the tenement buildings were in sagging, rickety disrepair. Tattered bits of laundry were strung from building to building, while whole families unlucky enough to miss cramming into a slum building lived in makeshift tents and cardboard shelters in vacant lots. Ragged, barefoot children seemed to be everywhere, and everywhere we were eyed with resentful looks that seemed almost palpable.

In this place of hunger and rags, I, who had only a few dollars in my pocket, was a rich American. I felt threatened and a bit guilty. By some accident of birth, I had it good and they had it bad. While this seemed obviously true, the contrasts between rich and poor, and the collision of two cultures, found poignant dramatization, for the Canal Zone cuts across Panama like a jeweled belt laid across a sodden gunny sack. I felt helpless in the face of what I saw.

I spoke of this to our friends. One of them shrugged his shoulders. "You get used to it," he said. That made me angry then. His tone seemed larded with a confidence that approached being self-righteous. But perhaps he was only protecting himself, as helpless to do much about the situation as I was. Still, it was no surprise to me that the Canal Zone came to symbolize for many Latin Americans an unconscionable intrusion on the part of the United States.

In Saint Thomas, we had met up with a Norwegian fishing boat and her crew of two who were delivering her to California. They happened to arrive and moor nearby in Cristobal, and we agreed to go through the locks with them in tandem. The idea was to raft the boats together in each lock, and this allowed for five of us to fend off and tend lines. It is advisable to have one person on each of the four lines needed in the locks, and it is a good idea to have a supply of battered fenders to protect the boat from possible contact with the lock walls. Since the Norwegian had plenty of fenders and a seemingly impregnable hull, we planned to raft *August Moon* on the outside, and keep our freshly varnished teak rails unblemished.

We had heard that the canal pilots who shuttle back and forth day after day enjoy the change of taking a cruising boat through. It provides a break from the difficult problem of navigating big ships in little water, with the chance of some amusement since most cruising people are crazy in a mild and interesting way.

A decent lunch was planned, some booze and ice

readied, and we looked forward to spending a day with our pilot. He came on board at 5:30 in the morning, and was not pleased to see us. He brought his own lunch and coffee, muttering something about the rotten food he usually got on small boats, which may well have been the case. In any event, he made it clear that he liked the power and glory of ships, in whose company *August Moon* was not. So we set off in sleepy-eyed silence for the Gatun Locks.

The Norwegian boat led the way, and we were glad to follow in her wake since they had been through before. While we were excited rather than alarmed about the journey, so many stories get tossed around about boats being damaged and the like, it was hard to know quite what to expect or what was expected of us. I had some vague image of overpowering floods of water tossing us helplessly about in the locks, or fumbling something in some way that would prove disastrous. As it was, we were moving in such proximity to ships that loomed over us, our vulnerability was very apparent.

The sun was bright before we reached the first of the locks. The steel gates, 68 feet high, were open and waiting for us to enter, which we did, nosing ahead very gingerly into the vast, dank cavern of the lock. The dripping stone walls rose up on either side higher than our main mast. We quickly rafted to the Norwegian boat, and got prepared for whatever was to happen next.

I generally think of a 46-foot boat as a pretty big piece of machinery. Even at sea with the whole horizon visible, one keeps a sense of her mass and size. But in the lock, which measures 110 feet by 1000 feet, she felt like a child's rubber duck floating in a bathtub. On looking up the grisly walls, you could see tiny heads with faces peering over the edge. They were in touch with our pilot by walkie-talkie radio who in turn yelled orders to us. Lines were passed, and as I glanced over our stern, I saw the enormous steel gates move soundlessly and ominously shut.

There was a clank which you could feel, and for a moment I experienced a sense of claustrophobia. Then the water started to flow in and we began to rise. The water flows from culverts beneath the surface which boils as when underwater springs disturb a lake. Since 26-million gallons of water are required to raise the level in a lock through 28 feet in about 8 minutes, the flow of water is swift and the boiling vigorous. If lines are improperly tended, if one of them is dropped, there is enough turbulence to swing the boat away from the dock wall as the water surges between the hull and the wall. On the other hand, it is not a great effort to keep sufficient pressure on the line as it slackens and is dragged on board through a fairlead. The trick is to keep up with it, not allowing either stern or bow to move far enough from the wall for a surge of water to come between.

Up we went, slowly, steadily, at about a yard per minute. When the water stopped flowing, we relaxed and looked around. Not much could be seen since our hull was not high enough to allow us to see over the lip of the dock. But the proportion of things was more comfortable now that the lock was full, as though we were floating in a big tank.

Then very slowly the great gate in front of us began to open. Its movement was so smooth and even, there was something ceremonial about it. We gathered our lines, and with the boats still rafted together we moved cautiously forward into the vast stone throat of the adjoining lock.

It was a bit like Dorothy and her friends clinging together for comfort as they walked gingerly through the palatial halls to meet the Wizard of Oz. The experience was a surreal one too, for while we had come up the walls of the first lock and were on the same water level as the second lock, the second lock was higher, ready to lift us another 28 feet, its wet walls towering over us as the first had done formerly. We moved forward all right, but with the strange sense that we were arriving back where we had started.

The great gates closed behind us, and the water began to flow. The same process was repeated, except that someone let a line get too slack. The sterns of the rafted boats began to swing outward, and it took some muscle to heave the weight of both boats back in line. The fenders scraped over the wet stone, and presently we were up.

Some dolphins, those magical comforters of cruising yachtsmen, had followed us into the first lock where they swam and tumbled as the fresh water flowed in. I feared they might drown or be hurt by being washed away when the lock was emptied. I asked our pilot who shrugged his shoulders and said nothing. I don't know what happened to them, but they didn't follow us into the second chamber.

The Gatun Locks are comprised of three chambers in succession, and between them they raise a vessel 85 feet above sea level. As we proceeded with growing confidence into the third lock of the series, I climbed out of the boat and scaled the wall in order to see what things looked like from the top.

Each lock had a double. That is to way, the three ascending locks we were dealing with were paralleled by another three so that traffic could move in either direction at once. From the top, they appeared as gigantic water troughs arranged in three descending steps. On the outer edges and running up the center dividing wall were railways on which tough little electric trains ran forward and back, moving improbably up the steep incline that connects a lower lock to its upper neighbor. These "mules" are used to pull ships into and through the locks, for were ships to use their own power they would be likely to get up a momentum and smash into the gates. As it is, the mules coax the ships forward so that they have almost no way or steerage on them, and they can be readily stopped by mules following behind.

Ships use their own power to come close to a lock, after which they are towed in. And the towing is necessary, for a large ship displaces so much water within the confines of the sealed lock that the displaced water would carry her back out were it not for the gentle forward pressure of the mules.

To look from the top of the Gatun Locks is an

amazing vision. The three lock chambers, each 1000 feet long, heavily weighted with millions upon millions of gallons of water, step grandly down to the waterway leading into the Caribbean. Misty green hills part for a vision of the port city, while, in the locks, great steel ships sit quietly like mechanical hens in a nest of water as they go up and down. Looking over the edge of the lock, I could see *August Moon* who looked no bigger than a wood shaving, the top of her mast unusually close to my nose. The thought struck me that if only I had a can of varnish and a brush, I could slap some on. But there was not time and, in truth, I couldn't have reached anyway.

Everything about the locks looks scrupulously clean. Hardware is maintained in prime condition. Although the first ship passed through the canal in 1914, locks retain a brand-new look, and function with impressive efficiency. Indeed, everything about the canal seemed so calm, I began to have apocalyptic fantasies of what would happen if one of the gates collapsed and a deluge from the lake swept down the steps carrying all before it. Since the Pacific Ocean is some feet higher than the Caribbean, I began to wonder what would happen if the plug were pulled. But having thought so much, I got back on board, helped get the two boats untied, and then we went under power into the Gatun Lake.

The artificial Gatun Lake has a shoreline of 1100 miles. The shipping channels are well marked, and small boats can push on under power at regular cruising speeds with the happy knowledge that the fresh water of the lake brings to a timely end all weed and crustaceans that have managed to pierce the bottom paint at sea.

Temperatures across the Isthmus stay close to 80 degrees year-round. This heat, larded with a weighty, oppressive humidity, makes one long for the ocean breezes ahead. And where the locks seem surreal, so does the lake. It is like the set for a Tarzan movie. The tops of trees that grew before the lake was filled still stick above the surface of the water, and close to these, weighty black freighters glide by. The vegetation on the banks is jungle-dense. There are alligators which I was disappointed to miss seeing, and much of the water's surface is dense with hyacinths, some 42 million of them needing to be annually destroyed lest they endanger navigation by fouling props. There is very little left to chance in the canal.

At the town of Gamboa, where the great Chagres River enters the lake, we were forced to stop and tie up while we waited for traffic to clear the Gaillard Cut which leads through mountains to the Pedro Miguel Locks.

It began to rain, thus assuring a humidity of 100 percent. We sweated, and the boat sweated, and I tried to write some letters which proved impossible until the page was mostly covered with a towel for my dripping hand and wrist to lean on.

I suppose the Gaillard Cut is the single most impressive aspect of the Panama Canal. At any rate, the existence of the canal depends on the fact that some eight miles of waterway were hewn and dug through solid mountainous rock. There is a vast cleft chiseled through mountains, in parts an upwardly widening ascension of rocky terraces that step to the sharp skyline far above.

While smaller ships moving in opposing directions can pass each other in the Cut, larger ships that require the deepest water in the channel must pass through singly. It turned out that we were waiting for a Russian warship to clear before proceeding.

One is dependent on the pilot throughout the entire navigation of the canal. But it is here, in the twisting Cut, that his good services are most clearly needed. The hills are set with markers which must be lined up to guarantee the safe passage of ships, while a system of warning signals are employed to avoid collision. Since the signals are particular to the needs of the canal, it would be hard indeed for a seaman not schooled in the system to attempt the passage.

As we passed through the Cut, gazing in awe and admiration at this spectacular achievement, even our taciturn pilot seemed moved enough to start speaking to us. But I kept thinking that it must have been here, the highest point on the Isthmus, that the Spanish explorer, Balboa, first gazed out over the Pacific Ocean. And I remembered the famous mistake that Keats made in his sonnet, "On First Looking into Chapman's Homer." He confuses Balboa with another explorer, Cortez, when he says:

> Or like stout Cortez when with eagle eyes
> He star'd at the Pacific—and all his men
> Look'd at each other with a wild surmise—
> Silent, upon a peak in Darien.

I was in Darien, and Keats being there too made it all the better.

We cleared the Cut and entered the Pedro Miguel Lock. This lock has only one descending chamber, a large drop of 31 feet. Going down is easier than coming up because the draining water is less anxious to push the boat against the walls or swirl it back. We were quickly through and into the small lake that leads for a mile and a half to the final, double set of locks, the Miraflores. These two chambers lowered us some 27 feet each, the needful depth varying depending on the Pacific tide at a given moment.

Then we were into the waterway leading to the Pacific and the port named after Balboa. We unlashed the two boats, and the Norwegian fishing boat that had accompanied us pushed off into the Pacific, hurrying to complete the delivery to California. We waved good-bye and never saw her again.

Our taciturn pilot was disgorged into a launch. Just as we were about to anchor in a group of yachts lying off Balboa, we spotted an English cutter lying ahead. She and her crew we had known in Puerto Rico. Such accidental meetings are one of the happiest aspects of cruising, so we pushed ahead to see if anyone was on board and to raft alongside.

We had just come through the Panama Canal, and by so doing had avoiding rounding the Horn and all of South America. We had cut 7,800 miles off our possible journey. It was three in the afternoon, eight and a half hours after we had weighed anchor in Cristobal in the Caribbean.

Our friends were on board, and as jubilant to see us as we to see them. We made good English black tea, calmed with some fresh milk which they had just gotten in Balboa. Powdered milk is better in tea than no milk, but you cannot have a good cup of tea without fresh milk.

Officialdom

THEY SEEM TO THINK you are up to something. It is
unclear to them why some people choose to go the
watery way around, and they suspect ulterior motives.
For which, I suppose, they earn their pay.

Booze and drugs are their prime suspicions when
it comes to cruising boats, and, just occasionally, they
are out to make some money for themselves.

Officials at ports in the vicinity of free ports where
liquor is sold at astonishingly low prices tend to look
very carefully at incoming yachts. They want to keep
a tight lid on smuggling and black-market dealings,
which is reasonable enough. Except that they can get
so unreasonable about it.

The *August Moon* was heading for Willemstad in
Curaçao after reaching for three days across the
trades from Puerto Rico. It had been smooth sailing
with every inch of sail set until the final night when it
really started to blow. The gennie halyard parted. A

little later, the mizzen staysail outhaul snapped a shackle. These things always happen at night.

We were reduced to staysail, main and mizzen. This was just as well, for the wind kept increasing, and the seas were getting very steep. We failed to spot the light we were looking for at the tip of Bonaire Island when we expected to see it. A couple of hours later, the light we did pick up and sail toward turned out to be the beacon at the airport. This was not good, especially in the middle of a mild gale, for we had hoped to pass to the east between the islands of Bonaire and Curaçao.

There was nothing for it but to make up our downwind drift by turning on the big diesel and smack into those stiff seas, for to turn and run before the wind would have driven us many miles in the wrong direction.

We got sail down, a difficult business with the boat plunging and the deck coursing with green water. We sheeted the main boom hard into the boom crutch as the sail was lowered, and then were able to lean on a stable boom to get the heavy, beating main furled safely.

The night got wilder, and it was my watch. It is always my watch when the going gets rough, but perhaps everyone thinks that. I surely did when I looked down the tossing companionway and saw billows of smoke. An electrical fire had started. The extreme motion of the boat had tossed two live wires together.

By the good luck that is yours when you really know your boat well, I guessed in a flash which wires

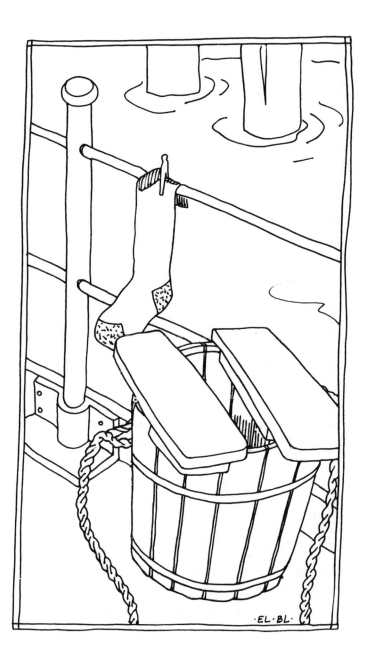

might have shorted and where to disconnect them. Roger and Jim were forward, trying to sleep, and I called them with blasts on the fog horn. They came staggering aft, coughing at the fearsome stink of burning wire, grabbing for fire extinguishers. No further harm was done, and we plunged on, taking water through hatch covers and seams. With all the effort that goes into making a boat watertight, I often wonder could less effort be any worse, for there is no such thing as a dry boat once the green water is coming aboard.

Then, in the galley which had been well enough stowed, a couple of lockers flew open, and out tumbled flour, tea, rice, salt, tapioca and detergent. It was a mess of messes in that sopping wet environment, and while we rescued what we could, the continual sluices of water created a vast sticky paste out of the staples.

It was in this condition, and aching from fatigue, that we safely entered Willemstad an hour after dawn. The medieval-looking Dutch buildings gave off a stately glow as we glided down the calm waterfront and docked. The big diesel stopped its throbbing, and we collapsed below to sleep on sopping wet bunks.

Then it arrived. Officialdom.

The beginning was mild enough. A chorus of ahoys from the dock managed to rouse us, grabbing for clothes and staggering around in the sodden mess trying to recover documents and passports. Two officials came on board and settled in the cockpit. We explained that we had been through a bad night and apologized for the mess. They were affable and unconcerned. Having stamped passports and checked documents, they wanted to see below.

There is something profoundly embarrassing, humiliating in the way of dirty laundry being aired, at having your boat inspected when it is not ship-shape, as surely we were not. Wet, pulpy charts were drooping from the chart table, foul-weather gear encrusted with salt was tossed on bunks, the food staples pasted on the galley sole looked like concrete waste around a construction zone. We were unkempt, unshaven and bent with fatigue. It was a sink of debauchery.

But to our amazement, the officials were full of awe and admiration. They inspected navigation equipment, praised the carpentry of the interior, the layout, and generally beamed as though they were prospective buyers with their minds made up. A fine ship, they said, and left with the casual remark that someone from customs would drop by later.

We collapsed.

About thirty minutes later, there was a loud hail, and the clatter of many feet coming on board. I almost awoke and staggered aft to find a whole bevy of officials, some black, some white, talking in Dutch and English and fingering this and that. They had come to welcome us, they said, to see our fine ship. And they proceeded to go over the documents the first officials had already stamped. They traipsed through that unholy mess, their official boots grinding the flour and tea and sugar and tapioca and rice and detergent solidified with salt and water that was some four inches thick into the main saloon and everywhere.

They were very good humored, and they asked us all the questions we had already answered as to our destination, where we came from, the sort of voyage we were making. They wished to know the specifications of *August Moon*, where she was built and by whom. They were pleased to discover she had been built in Holland, and with a certain patriotism glowing—for here we were in the Netherlands Antilles—their inspection tour intensified until they had remarked over every square inch that was visible above water.

By the time they left, my fatigue was burning like an incandescent light so that sleep seemed hopeless, and, while the others dozed off forward, I settled in the main saloon and mixed a strong drink of scotch.

It was at this point the customs inspectors arrived, and, whereas their front-runners had cantered through our mess with esprit, these two fellows looked grimly at the floor and then with furrowed brows at the bottle of scotch perched on the saloon table.

I thought they wanted a drink, and offered them one. It turned out they did not want a drink, and they did not want me to have a drink either. While it was true that the sun was not yet over the yardarm, this sort of puritanism is rarely found in the Caribbean.

Where did the liquor come from? they wanted to know. I pointed to our liquor locker. Where was it purchased? Puerto Rico, Saint Thomas, Saint Croix, somewhere like that, I replied. How much was on board?

I opened the locker and showed them a few open bottles, rum, gin, vermouth. It was an innocent enough sort of vision, and hardly the hoard that might inspire fantasies of black-market dealings, even in the most suspicious mind.

They gave instructions that the locker be closed, and padlocked so that they might seal it. Since there was no means of securing the locker short of employing a carpenter to fit it for a padlock, they relented and settled for my promise that the locker would not be opened while we were in port. If we required liquor, we could go ashore and buy it. They made a cursory search of the vessel, and finding nothing of interest, they left.

This struck me as a ridiculous state of affairs, the letter of some law being carried to tiresome lengths. They had told me where to purchase liquor on shore, so, by way of showing good faith, I wandered in their tracks onto the dock. Just as I cleared the boat, another group of officials drove up in a jeep and swarmed down the ladder for a slight-seeing tour. I ignored them, pretending I was just a passer by, and figured that the two men asleep below could deal with them.

About an hour passed before I returned, laden

with supplies, and feeling profoundly ready for sleep. The sun was high and hot as I lurched along the waterfront to where *August Moon* was moored.

Except that she was not. She was not there. I looked up and down the harbor. There was no sign of her beloved sticks. I recalled specifically the bollards to which she had been tied and the antique top-heavy building opposite. She was gone.

It is one thing to have a floating home, and quite another to have it float away without you. Now that it was lunch hour, the docks were deserted. There was no one to ask, even in Dutch which I did not speak. So I stood there, clutching the sagging sack of supplies, against this deserted stage-set of old Holland, and wondered what the weight of officialdom had managed. There was no glimmer of her white hull in the dark water.

In the most literal sense, I did not know where to turn. Nothing I could think of gave me the slightest clue as to why or where she might have been moved. So, like the fighting bull who selects a portion of the ring near the barrier when he recognizes what dangerous terrain he has entered, I settled down by the bollard and gazed at the dark, blank area of water where she should have been.

I had been slouching there for some time when a tugboat came down the channel. The men on board waved and shouted incomprehensibly. They brought the tug nearer. Jacht, Jacht, they yelled in Dutch, pointing upstream and waving. How they might have known me from Adam, I could not imagine. But I pointed at myself, and then upstream, and they nodded and yelled, Jacht, and sailed on.

So I picked up my sad sack and took my way along the docks upstream, for that seemed as sensible as staring at the water. And sure enough, about a half-mile upstream in a turning basin near a shipyard were the familiar varnished sticks. The deck was swarming with welders and carpenters working on the hull.

It turned out that, in my absence, a tug had smashed into our port quarter. It split the teak cap rail, stove in the steel hull, and mangled the after pulpit. It was an official tug which officially admitted its trangressions. But even more unusual, it provided ready access to workmen and repair, so they towed the boat upstream, and within two hours of strikingly intensive labor had made everything right, except for the addition of varnish. My vision of officials brightened.

But that vision was to be short-lived, for a few weeks later we were in Mexican waters where the port of entry we selected was Salina Cruz. It might have been tagged appropriately with Dante's dire warning from *The Inferno:* Abandon Hope All Ye Who Enter Here.

Until we entered Salina Cruz, we had been in and out of several Latin American ports without trouble. Our preceding port had been Quepos in Costa Rica. There, after we had been anchored off for a bit, an official rowed out in a dinghy. He smiled, spoke no English, managed to request a beer, stamped our passports, had another beer, and rowed off smiling under his big floppy sunhat. It was all very civilized in a casual, tropical way.

The sailing directions indicated that one should anchor in the outer harbor of Salina Cruz and await officials. This we did. When no officials appeared, and there was no sign of life around, we weighed anchor as evening approached and moved through the narrow channel to the inner harbor in the hope of getting some information.

There was a dock area to port, and another dock area to starboard. As we slowly circled, wondering what to do and where to go, a slew of uniformed officials appeared on the starboard dock. They waved vigorously, running about in some excitement, indicating clearly that we should dock to starboard. Since no one appeared to port, it seemed reasonable enough to do as we were bid.

It was all very queer in an indefinable though slightly sinister way. The curious neglect when we lay in the outer harbor, now this sudden scurry of activity. A small army had suddenly mobilized, and we were the target of their attentions. As lines were tossed ashore, a fat one pointed at me and yelled, Castro Ruz, Castro Ruz.

You Castro amigo? he asked as we tied up, pointing clearly to my beard. It was a blond beard and fairly short, one that in no way might call up Castro's image. So I smiled and shook my head. But he went on calling me Castro Ruz anyway. He was very loud, laughed a lot, and liked to play with the revolver hanging from his holster. He wanted to see below.

Several officials came on board to look around. Instead of stamping our passports, they took them away with them, indicating that the port was closed for the night, and the port captain would look at our papers in the morning. We were instructed to remain on board, not to go into town even for a meal, which we had dearly hoped for. Besides, they indicated, the port gates were locked. They pointed this out. Everything would be taken care of in the morning.

When morning came, Roger, having a little more Spanish than Jim or me, went to deal with the officials. As the two of us worked on some repairs, I was surprised to see two officials, one of whom was the fat one who told us his name was Mauricio, lounging around the boat. They seemed to have nothing else to do, and sat on the dock, peering as we worked, talking loudly. I asked why they stayed so long. They joked and said they were there to make sure we did not try to leave. I reminded them that they were holding our passports. This made them laugh a lot.

When Roger returned, he told us that the officials planned to hold us because we had no dispatch papers from our previous port, Quepos. He had already sent a telegram to Quepos requesting them. I thought of the fellow in the floppy hat who had drifted out to stamp our passports. It did not seem very likely that much would stir on the Quepos end.

As indeed it did not, even with the supplication of

further telegrams. There was nothing for it but to
sand and varnish and try to be patient under the constant watch of Mauricio and his cohorts whose bawdy
humor seemed more and more threatening as their
watch continued.

We learned, as the idle days of captivity went on,
that there were two ports. One was a town port under
the authority of a town captain, and the other, the
one we were in, was a free port which had its own
captain, and it was now that he chose to take a vacation. It had been a matter of going to port or starboard as we entered the inner harbor. Clearly we had
made a sad choice.

But, just as we really knew very little, we also did
not really know if our free-port captain was on vacation because we had never met him. When we went to
try and get things straight, the door to his office was
always closed. We were dealt with by underlings,
none of whom spoke English and all of whom indicated difficulty with our attempts at Spanish.

There was some sly talk from Mauricio that perhaps we had stolen the vessel, for, after all, we did not
have papers. Perhaps, he suggested, the case fell
under the jurisdiction of the town captain. Perhaps
we should speak to him. I could not tell whether
Mauricio was trying to be helpful or if in some insidious way he was trying to complicate the issue. In any
event, a pattern emerged to engage our days, a futile
pattern as only Kafka truly speaks of.

Every morning we would plead our case and present all the papers we had for approval in the office

of the free-port captain. They would ponder the matter as though they had until that moment been unaware of it. Then they would raise some insignificant question, always having difficulty understanding our Spanish, and mention that the captain was on vacation. Perhaps, they suggested, this is a matter best handled, under the circumstances, by the town captain.

Always one of us stayed on board to protect the vessel from pilfering—we were ready for anything at this point—while the other two would walk through the dusty park and the fly-buzzing markets of the crumbling town to the office of the town captain. By the time we got there, it would be noon, and so we had to wait until after the captain had his lunch and his siesta before we could see him. Since there were generally several people waiting ahead of us, it was close to four o'clock before he proferred some judgment on the minor issue, the upshot of which was always that we should once more appeal to the office of the free-port captain.

By the time we had dragged through the heat and dust of the town and the couple of miles back to the free port, the office was just on the point of closing, and we were invited to come back the following morning, and so forth, until we became paranoid, and a bit frightened, and cross with each other.

It is a bad thing when friends became cross with each other. To argue and disagree is healthy, if painful. But to be cross is lamentable. Ours had always been a happy ship as ships go. We got along, liking each other well enough to sail together, and we let each other go our separate ways when on land. But now we were hatched up like rats and silly things began to go wrong.

For example, I got a late start on varnishing one morning, and when the hot noon sun stood overhead the varnish had not adequately set so that it blistered into a bubbling mess. This was discouraging. I began to feel unwell, becoming angry at Roger when he insisted I had a headache because my varnishing was bad. While headaches can certainly arise from such things, I discovered a few hours later that I had picked up a severe case of tourista, with its dire and tiresome results.

Unfortunately, Roger had carelessly put something undigestable in the head—a thoughtlessness quite untypical of him, so that the head was out of order just when I needed to spend frequent amounts of time there. It was up to Roger to fix it, but he was cross too and refused to take on the task.

Buckets are not bad things to use, I suppose. But in port they are difficult, particularly under the nosey, roistering Mauricio whose raucous laugh and small talk were a continual presence as he lounged on the dock playing with his gun, gleefully observing our growing despair.

Day after day passed in this absurd pattern. A week went by. We speculated that what they really wanted from us was money, to be bribed. Since we had money on board, I was all for paying up and getting out. The idea was rejected by the other two who outvoted me with a moral fervor I felt quite unwarranted under the circumstances. Both Roger and Jim had been divinity students, and perhaps that is why they felt so strongly. We more or less ran the ship on democratic principles, so I had no recourse but to tag along with the majority, and my bucket.

We began to fantasize that perhaps we could escape at night, sail away from this terrible place. If we could provision adequately, we could sail clear of Mexican waters and reach California without touching another Mexican port where we might be apprehended again. But, of course, they had our passports. So that was hopeless.

The grinning Mauricio must have read our thoughts. "A boat like you," he said. "We have it for six months. They try to escape. Boom. The big gun." He pointed to what from a distance appeared to be a World War II antiaircraft gun. It was mounted on a bluff overlooking the outer harbor. Then he added, in his sly way, "There are patrol boats."

There probably were patrol boats, and they probably would use the big gun, for such events would give some meaning to the lives of these loitering, petty officials. The chance to use the big gun would be a benchmark in their idle days to come. They were puffed-up tyrants in this crumbling town whose inhabitants were primarily Indians.

It was at this point we met an American, a padre working at the local Catholic church. Word had reached him that we were having difficulties. He came to the boat and offered to do what he could for

us. At the very least, his fluent Spanish and his position in the community might be aids in discovering
what was really going on. He agreed to join us in
speaking to the port captain who, it was now said,
would return from his vacation in two days.

This was a gladdening thought, and, oddly enough,
as our spirits lifted a bit, Mauricio's spirits seemed to
sag a little. "Yes," Mauricio sighed when he spoke of
the padre, "he is a very good man. He will help make
things clear."

It seemed as though Mauricio saw that the end
might be in sight. He had been having so much fun
guarding the ship of the two norte americanos and an
amigo of Castro Ruz. It had quite singled him out
among his brother officials. It had made him special,
and now that would soon end. His oppressive brag-
gadocio subsided when he was alone with us at least,
unobserved by his brethren.

He wanted to be friendly, telling of his wife and
children, how poor they were, especially in comparison to people who sailed in ships with radios and batteries. "So many batteries for one person," he said
when he saw me stowing spare ones in a locker. I told
him that they were not mine, that they belonged to
the ship. It was clear that Mauricio would like some
of our batteries.

Now it so happened that this day was my birthday,
my twenty-first birthday. I badly wanted to go into
town that evening to celebrate by buying a drink, a
legal drink. I had hoped to be in the United States for
this event where I would surely have been asked to
produce identification to prove my age which would

have burnished my pleasure. If I had to forgo that, I was certainly not going to spend my birthday under armed guard, not if I could help it.

It was the pattern at evening that Mauricio packed up his guns and went home. The gates to the port were locked, and we were not meant to scale them. When I had washed and put on clean clothes, I placed half a dozen batteries in a paper bag and, as I stepped ashore, gave them to Mauricio.

He was delighted, setting aside his rifle so as to more readily remove the batteries from the bag and count them. I explained that I was giving him a present because today was my birthday and I wished to go into town and have a drink.

To this he was quite agreeable, and I left him sitting on the dock where he had settled down to build his batteries into a little pyramid.

It felt good to be off and alone. I knew the path into town all too well, for our days of running from one set of officials to another had made us familiar with it. We had shopped for supplies and wandered around the markets where we became used to being stared at as strangers, the only norte americanos, the only white people apart from the padre. But I had not been there alone, and I had not been there at night.

Still, the bribe had worked. I wished we had bribed all of the officials ten days earlier and gotten it over with. Then, going through the little park as the evening shadowed in, it occurred to me that I was really alone, and in strange, possibly dangerous terrain. It was then I heard a burst of rifle fire behind me. I leaped behind a tree and felt that little surge of energy that rushes up before fear sets in.

Through the gloom, I could make out a figure running, heard yells and a further rifle shot. It was, of course, Mauricio, puffing along, calling my name, his fat, sweaty face beaming as he caught up with me.

He had come to understand, he said, he had spoken with the others on the boat, that this was a grande birthday. He was going to buy me a drink and share my coming into manhood.

Since he had the gun, I was literally his prisoner. I agreed to drink with him, and was in a way relieved that I had some company, even Mauricio, although I was not fond of him or his gun, and I mistrusted his new pleasantries as much as I found his earlier behavior sinister.

He took me to a canteena where he said he would teach me how to drink tequila. He would pay for everything. And we walked on, his rifle carelessly thrown over his shoulder, the pockets of his pants bulging with the batteries I had given him. We were, for now, amigos.

The bar, the canteena, was not quite like any bar I had been in before. It was a large room with metal tables and chairs scattered about without much order. At the far end was a long wooden bar without bar stools. There was a ceiling-high mirror behind it, cracked and marred with several small holes that made me think of rifle fire. Built onto one end of the bar was a urinal, a working one, I gathered, as a huge Indian moved away from using it.

Perhaps half a dozen Indians were standing around the bar, one of them picking his teeth with a hunting knife. They drank slowly and stared at me. At me, the only white person, with longish hair and a beard made blond by exposure to sun and salt water, wearing a blue-and-white-striped shirt and white canvas sailing pants. I never in my life felt more noticeable and vulnerable.

Mauricio was in fine form, enjoying the situation enormously, taking advantage of my vulnerability as his captive. He began to show these fellows what a big man he was.

I was from a magnificent yacht sailing around the world, he told them. He, Mauricio, was holding the entire ship captive until certain irregularities had been investigated. Tonight was my birthday when he would teach me how to drink tequila like a man.

The dark, unspeaking men formed a semicircle around where I stood at the bar. Mauricio ordered the tequila and it came, raw as benzine, in two large tumblers without ice. The bartender slid them up the bar, then handed us some slices of lime and a bowl of salt.

To this day, I cannot remember if one is meant to eat the salt before drinking tequila and then bite the lime, or eat the lime and drink before taking the salt, or eat both the lime and salt before washing it back. But Mauricio showed me the way, swallowing his tumbler of gut-cutting booze in one gulp before turning to watch my effort.

I brought the glass near my nose. As drinkers go, I

fall into the sipping category, not the gulping one. I wanted to taste this stuff that smelled like lighter fluid. But when I paused, there was a slight stiffening in the circle of men around me. So I gulped. It hit my stomach like a water hammer, and I filled my mouth with either salt or lime to deaden the taste of it.

The Indians relaxed. I had passed the test. But Mauricio, in his winsome way, decided to prolong it by buying me two more glasses of knockout drops. By the time we sat down at a table to drink some innocent beer, the room had taken on a gentle motion. I noticed that the big cracked mirror had scrawled on it, in what looked like lipstick, Jesus amor Maria. One of the Indians, the biggest of them with long, tangled, black hair, was leaning drunkenly at the bar, and staring in my direction in a way that made me feel very uncomfortable.

A couple of Mauricio's friends had joined us, so there was a great deal of talk in Spanish that went far too fast for me to follow, although I gathered that Mauricio was once more rehearsing, in increasing detail, the story of how he had captured the "August Moon." The table piled up with beer bottles and the evening swayed along.

I hardly cared. It was my twenty-first birthday. This was exactly what I wanted. Until I felt, looming over me like some great gothic figure in a dream, a malign presence. I looked up and saw the big Indian standing beside me. He was swaying from booze, and it may have been that his body was already slowly, slowly descending.

He reached out to touch my hair. "I want to kiss you," he said. "I think you are Jesus Christ."

Even before I could pull back, his effort to reach me had overtoppled him. He crashed, unconscious, onto the table which collapsed, sending beer bottles smashing and fizzing across the floor.

At a glance, Mauricio and I decided it was time to go. It was our only moment of complicity. He gathered up his cap and rifle. We left the Indian lying on the floor, the upturned table partly on top of him and puddles of beer around his head. Then we went out into the dank, hot tropical night.

The following day Mauricio did not appear. The padre who had befriended us arrived in the afternoon. We took our papers to the office of the port captain, happy to have a good translator with us.

It was not necessary. Whereas before we had to struggle with a little Spanish to officials who had no English, now the same officials conversed in fluent English. The door to the inner office was open to where the port captain was working. He was able to see us right away. He went over our papers. He explained in English that it was regrettable we had departed from Quepos without correct papers, but, since we had all of the correct papers from Panama, there was no doubt as to our integrity. He provided us with sailing papers and returned our passports. Everything was in order.

We thanked the padre, and ran down the dock, casting off lines and pushing the boat away to open water before we had the engine going. In five minutes we were out of that harbor and out into the big, beautiful sea.

We had no further trouble in Mexican ports, and we expected none when we arrived in California and entered San Diego. It was ten o'clock at night. There was a message waiting from Dr. R. S. Harrison, the boat's owner, that we should proceed directly to Los Angeles, but, for reasons that were not clear, the officials would not allow us to do this, possibly because we had already entered San Diego harbor. We would have to go through customs on the following morning.

The officials asked had we liquor on board, and they were shown the meager supply we had. Then they asked about drugs. Since this was a doctor's boat, she was well stocked with first-aid supplies which included morphine. They asked where the morphine was, and I took them to the medicine locker in the head where I showed them a small, soggy cardboard box that contained a half-dozen unopened glass phials.

When they saw this, their anger was so explosive that I thought they might do us physical harm. They seized the box from my hands, asking did I not know this was illegal? How dare we sail into American waters and declare such a thing!

I explained that we were completing a voyage of several months' duration, and that we necessarily carried basic medical supplies for emergencies. The doctor had wisely left morphine on board which was, of course, legally obtained, and we were not trying to smuggle since here it was declared.

Any explanation only heated their anger. They confiscated the morphine and forbade us to leave the vessel until it had been properly inspected the next day.

We were outraged and dismayed that U. S. officials would behave in such a manner to the crew of an American yacht who were clearly cooperating and showing good faith. Nothing had been said by way of rudeness or disrespect to garner such a response. It was puzzling and disheartening to arrive in home waters to such a welcome. There was nothing to do but wait till morning for further inspections.

The two plain-clothed officials who arrived the following day were not pleased to see us. To call them taciturn would be to call them sweet. They were not even passingly polite as they began an exhaustive search of the vessel that stretched into hours.

Every nook and cranny was fingered, pillows punched, boxes opened. There was no place they did not search. *August Moon* had a sizable deck aft plate fastened down with some thirty-odd screws. It was clear that these screws had not been touched since the boat was built, for there were layers of paint built up on them.

What, the officials wanted to know, was concealed under there? I told them nothing was concealed as they could see if they would crawl aft over the engine and look. This they would not do, and they forced us to clear the paint from the screws and undo every one of them, a half-hour job.

I had the impression, by this time, that they were out to get us in some malevolent way. It was annoying that the deck plate would have to be stripped and repainted before being replaced. And they were dismayed, I think, to find nothing under the plate, for their eagerness to get their noses into the after deck was matched by a surly disappointment when they discovered nothing.

They began tapping the masts, wanting to know were they hollow, which of course they were. I began to fear they might make us unstep them in order to peek up the bottom. They did not, but they renewed their search, pulling up the floorboards so as to snoop into the depth of the bilges which, after the various storms and perturbations of our voyage, were in great need of cleaning. In this soil they buried themselves, coming up with a can of beans that had escaped the galley, a flyswatter missing these several months, and lo! a bottle of scotch. They emerged from their oil trench waving it like a victor's trophy over their heads, gasped for air like fish out of water, and dove down again. They paddled about, churning the bilge water with their finney hands, and managed to latch onto a bottle of brandy.

Well, they were so transparent in their combination of glee and weak-kneed attempt at judicial propriety, it was sickening. They actually, having found the liquor as they did, asked had we declared these two bottles. It was so apparent that the bottles had somehow gone astray, that we knew nothing about them, one was hard put to respond. When I considered the intensity of their search, the inconvenience to us, their rudeness, and our clear open-handedness, I could only laugh. "Believe me," I said, "if I had known they were there, they'd be empty by now."

Levity, alas, is a serious misdemeanor when expressed to petty officials. There is no way one can cower sufficiently to please them. As their sweaty brows glowered in an attempt to assert their authority, I explained that the owner entertained a lot and stowed liquor under the port berth. Clearly in stormy weather, and we had been knocked flat on at least one occasion, the forgotten bottles had flipped down into the bilge. I was not joking when I said we had not known they were there.

But they, it turned out, were not joking either. They made threats, saying that this was grounds for confiscating the vessel. They said they were going to take us to court over it. And they did.

In these days when courts are so overburdened as to beggar justice, we appeared on a charge of smuggling into the United States a quart of scotch and a quart of brandy. We were arraigned, tried, and found guilty. We were fined and the liquor, whose existence we were unaware of, was confiscated.

I hope the judge enjoyed it. It was a good French brandy imported from the Champagne country.

Food Aboard

ICE IS THE TROUBLE. Ice and the difficulty of refrigeration. Now there is a philosophy among small-boat sailors that the best answer is to open a can of goo and pour it over something worse. People just give up.

Power-boat sailors whose very lives depend on banks of batteries have solved the ice problem by installing deep freezers and refrigerators. But how they cope with the pressing and continual bite of corrosion, electrical failure, and electrolysis seems such a treadmill that I would as soon forgo their chill.

The large, professionally crewed sailboat can afford both the space and maintenance associated with electrical gadgets. But the small boat, especially the cruising boat, is best without such paraphernalia. Simple rigs, simple decks, and simple galleys are the best guarantees of days spent sailing.

Ice is not so bad, especially when used in a well-insulated icebox. And when the icebox is used carefully—that is to say, not opened and closed every five minutes—a good solid block will do the trick for several days. But chipping ruins it, and this is a problem when people insist on having ice in their drinks. To carry a second block for chipping only is good, but best of all is to adopt the practice of the English who like to taste their scotch, rolling it over tongues that are not anesthetized from ice.

English drinkers, admittedly, are used to a climate so dank and cool that ice is to be avoided, but when they colonized half the hot part of the globe, they took their scotch along and sipped it warm. It all depends on what one is used to.

Ice, of course, becomes an impossible luxury on a seagoing voyage, and I suppose it was under these conditions that dry biscuits and tough, salted beef became cruising staples. A spartan attitude developed that food aboard was for survival only, and somehow that has crept into present times when canned meats and vegetables are remarkably good, if lacking the finesse of fresh food.

A friend of mine recently crewed on a boat going from Los Angeles to Tahiti, and she was dismayed to discover that the owners had provisioned almost exclusively with canned chili and beans. That is what they ate for lunch and dinner throughout the days and weeks until they made landfall in the South Pacific. The crew was sick to the point of mutiny, and fought over a single can of clam chowder.

I suspect that a sort of laziness has snuck into the galley, laziness and a lack of imagination in the face of obvious difficulties. But the point is that cooking,

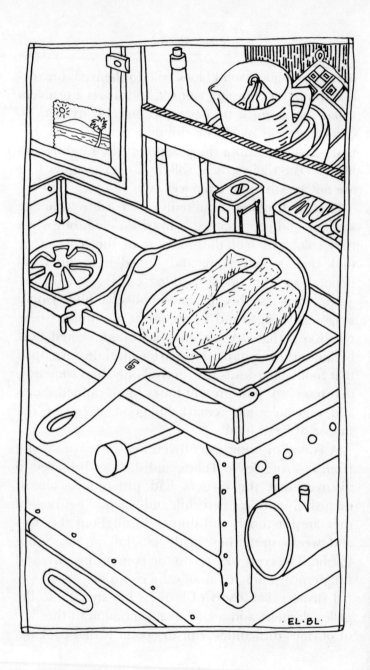

EL·BL·

along with reading, chamber music, gardening and sailing, is one of the fine ways to ease the soul and delight the senses. It is one of the kinder means of balancing a woeful century.

Every meal should be a feast—not in the amount but in the quality and preparation. It is just as easy to do things well as to do them badly, and when the results are succulent and delicious, doing things well becomes easier still. Which is to say, cooking is a philosophy, a way of thinking about things.

The cook who opens a can of beans and brings it to the boil over a burner adheres to one philosophy. The cook who uses the same skillet and burner to gently sauté a fresh fillet of fish, herbed with some marjoram, and salt and pepper, then removes the fish the moment the flesh is set through, deglazes the pan with some white wine before pouring the residue over the fish as a simple sauce, adheres to quite another.

I fell in with that way of dealing with fish from a young Mauritian sailor who happened to be standing on the dock in Saint Thomas as we were off for a shakedown cruise in the British Virgins. Having nothing better to do, he helped us cast off lines and then hopped aboard when we said there was plenty of room. He spoke French and was drifting his way around the world, crewing on one boat or another as the opportunity arose.

When we anchored that evening, he slipped overboard with a speargun and came back with a fine brown grouper, one of the great fishes for eating. In a flash he filleted it and went to work in the galley as

I watched. It had never occurred to me that such a delicious result could be achieved with such impressive ease.

Somehow I had convinced myself that good cooking required the ministrations and secret rituals that go on in expensive French restaurants. Nor had I considered that fresh seafood was there for the taking. My sailing had been so tied up with navigation and maintenance, plus the excitement of cruising, I had not considered the joy of taking time to fish and prepare a fine meal while lying at anchor in a good sheltered bay.

Thereafter I took to skin-diving and came back with tuna, lobster, bass, and felt very good about it. And, as happens often, when things go very well, I got somewhat cocky about it. Perhaps an element of greed took over. In any event, I caught too many fish.

We had anchored off a small island, and the two of us who were on board went skin-diving for supper. There was a steady current which carried us a good quarter of a mile from the boat until we came over a reef that was clouded with all manner of fish. They flashed this way and that in silver swirls and a turbulence of color. There were enormous submarine fish that hung like gleaming blimps in the water. They seemed too massive to float or swim, and when a spear was shot at them, it bounced off their tough armored sides with a ping that echoed underwater as a silver scale or two fluttered slowly down. They lazed about unperturbed.

The two of us took about a half-dozen small fish

each, and in the process lost the spears from our guns. The retaining strings broke, and the spears sank to depths we could not dive. But we had plenty of fish, strung through the gills in a bunch and towed close to our feet by a string that I tied around my waist. We began the long swim back to the anchored yacht.

We swam side by side, our faces down in the water as we breathed through snorkels, watching the undulations of sand and reef ride slowly under. When my companion touched my arm, he said he had just seen a shark. I spun around 360 degrees in the water, searching the smooth water for the sign of a dorsal fin. There was no sign of one, and we swam on.

Later, we both admitted that it had occurred to us to drop the fish bobbing behind us. But we were proud of our catch and were not about to part with it. So we swam on, taking turns to scan the small horizon we could see, dipping down from time to time to peer through the clear water into the shadows. We saw nothing and swam on.

When it hit us, it was as though we saw in some inner eye exactly what was going on, even though in the thrashing of white water and blood we could in fact see nothing. Our bodies were thrown apart as something ripped between us, scarring like sandpaper. I think my body actually left the water—and surely I wished it had. Before I reentered I tore the string from about my waist and cast the fish loose.

The trouble was we could see nothing from the surface, and, on the theory that it is better to know than not know, dove down, needing to see and wanting to see nothing. What we saw were the fish about fifteen feet downstream. They had been ripped in half, a smoky trail of blood puffing from them. Beyond them, circling with a flick of his tail, was a full-grown shark, clearly about to attack again.

There is something about the motion, shape and visage of a shark that fully explains at a glance why we use the work "shark" only with prejudice. The blunt determination of his motion, the utter lack of sensibility and the ignorance of all other concern but his own are repulsive. He is no different than the sea, or anything else in it, but he strikes so profoundly at some archetypal memory, it was perhaps to avoid such things that we came on land in the first place.

It is said that in such desperate moments there is no time for terror. This is untrue. There was ample, luxurious time, a lifetime wrapped in a few seconds for utter panic and terror. As he came at us again, I turned my shaking, unarmed gun on him. It was a hopeless gesture, but it was something.

Both of us back-paddled upstream as he sailed toward us. Just as he gathered speed for his attack, he paused. He was downstream from us, and now the remains of the bleeding fish were downstream from him. The current saved us for, in a flash, he spun toward the blood and tore at the remnants of the fish. He snatched and shook them like a dog might. There was a pale flurry of entrails, and then they were gone.

I did not look anymore. We both surfaced and began the slow, leaden swim back to the boat who seemed so far away we could never reach her. Exhausted from terror, and in continual fear of further attack, there was nothing for us to do but swim on. We were both aware that, were it to happen now, miles from help, no one would ever know. I resolved not to put myself in such a position again.

When we did reach the boat, we were so weak from fear that we had to pull and push each other up the ladder and onto the safety of the deck. We collapsed in the warm sun, lying silently for over half an hour. There was a raw stripe grazed on my side where his body had contacted mine.

Sharks tend to be fairly predictable in their attack patterns, and if you leave a trail of blood through shark-infested waters, as we did, you can expect trouble. Thereafter we were careful to skin-dive close to the dinghy and get fish out of the water before their bleeding could excite any passing shark. It is one thing to eat fish, and quite another to be eaten by them.

Shellfish are safer, especially when taken from the clean shores of islands off the New England coast. Steamers are easiest to get. They live around the half-tide mark, buried in sand, and give their presence away by a characteristic hole in the sand and occasional jets of water, which is why down-east in Maine the natives call them piss clams.

They can be dug by hand, but a clam fork makes the work much easier when one forkful will often uncover several clams at once. Breaking the shells of some clams when digging is unavoidable, for very little pressure from the tangs of a fork will do it. Broken clams are best discarded, but since seagulls will get them, nothing is wasted.

Once enough clams are collected, it is a good idea to leave them in a bucket of fresh seawater for at least several hours so that they have time to disgorge their sand. In Maine, where I did a lot of clamming, I used to keep them in a slated wooden box which floated at the surface of the water and was attached to a mooring. Under such conditions they filter merrily and stay alive indefinitely. I was surprised to observe that after several days their shells, which were bluish brown when dug, turned white in the continual flush of clean water. When some were needed for a meal, I would row out and take as many as were wanted, and I got into the habit of replacing the clean ones with freshly dug ones, like a revolving credit charge, because it was such a pleasure to eat clams without grit in them.

Crab and lobster and mussels can be kept underwater in such boxes also. So, one summer in Maine, I had a line of boxes floating from the mooring, their inhabitants filtering and cleansing in the clean, cool water. It was a perfect larder. We collected when we could, and ate what we needed.

Steamer clams have a delicate flavor which I find best enhanced by steaming them in a pot with a cup or so of white wine and water. Chopped onion, bayleaf and parsley thrown into the liquid helps, and when the clams have opened after five to ten minutes of steaming, they are ready to be served. It is best to eat them out of the shell, pulling out the meat and stripping away the tough skin that covers their little necks. A quick swirl in a finger bowl filled with the cooking juices helps remove any sand that might be present. It is hard to stop eating them. And when the last one is had, the juices are there for drinking and dunking bread in.

The fresh, flavorful clam juice that results from the steaming is a wonderful thing to poach fish in, should that be your next course. At home it freezes well, while at sea there is always more to be had.

Steamers are fine for use in spaghetti sauces and chowders, but the best clams for chowders are hen clams. They have a stronger and sweeter flavor. These large clams, some eight inches in length, are hard to come by because they flourish just beyond the lip of the very lowest spring tides and are always covered by water. To find them, the surface of the water must be very smooth so that when wading you can see through to their crater in the sand. After that the fun begins, for once the clamming fork is pushed in, there is stir and turmoil, and all visibility is lost. One has to work by feel.

Hen clams have a foot that reaches down into their bed. As soon as they are disturbed, they pull themselves down quite powerfully, and a fair tug-of-war ensues before they are wrenched out. Even then they are easy to lose in the swirl of muddy water.

They are an exciting prize, and large enough so that a half-dozen will do for a big chowder. One opens them with a knife like an oyster. Their insides, a messy combination of belly, intestine and muscle are not a fine sight for the squeamish. But they are good food, and when the belly is slit and cleaned out, the meat around the rim of the shell preserved, there remains the muscle that opens and closes the two complimenting shells keeping them safe from all but us. It is the same muscle that we take from the scallop, while throwing away so much else that should not be thrown away. But the hen clam has a much larger muscle which is tough and not considered edible by many people. If, however, it is marinated and stewed gently in its own juices, it becomes tender enough to use in traditional scallop recipes where it proves equally succulent. A few minutes with a toothpick after eating takes care of leftovers.

Mussels are surely the most neglected shellfish native to the United States, and consequently they are the most plentiful of all. Americans seem to fear them almost as much as the French delight in them, possibly because their flesh is startlingly orange in color, their taste particular, and their physiognomy a seeming replica of the human vagina. Americans are still touchy when it comes to sex. But mussels are very good, combining well with Provencal flavors into soups, or chopped and sautéed with herbs and bread crumbs before being baked in their own shells. A handsome dish.

Perhaps it is their plentifulness that makes Americans shy away from mussels, just as the pilgrim fathers are said to have done with lobsters, for in colonial days lobsters were so plentiful that they crawled about even in rock pools where they could be taken by hand. What we now regard as an elegant dish was then regarded as unworthy stuff for an important dinner. Taste is fashion.

All shellfish can be dangerous, for they take in through their valves whatever polluting stuff may be in the water. The New England states are strict in their posting of warnings on beaches where there may be a health hazard. Generally such warnings are given in waterways near major cities, places where cruising boats rarely are. But occasionally a red tide sweeps the coast and stops short all taking of shellfish, for they become temporarily poisonous.

Red tide is so-called because of the enormous numbers of dinoflagellates that flourish when water is warm, their presence giving the sea a reddish tinge. The problem is that when we ingest shellfish that are taken from a red tide, we get poisoned. But once the water clears, the shellfish clear themselves. Their flesh does not become contaminated, and they flush clean.

On the West Coast the problem is a little more subtle, for here the water warms and provokes the red tide throughout the summer season. What is headline news in New England is a more continual and insinuating possibility in California. The Indians were so aware of this danger that they are said to have posted warnings for each other, and folklore has it that the months with an "R" in them are safe for shellfishing, while the warmer months of May through August are likely to be dangerous. It is a matter of water temperature.

This business of foraging for seafood and learning to cook it takes a little time. But once some experience is raked up, you remember which rocky point is good for musseling, or which beach is good for clams, so that on your next passage you have local knowledge. It has much to do with what is joyful about cruising— being in touch with wind and weather, keeping the boat floating and moving safely on.

While it is good to have some canned food tucked away for emergencies, I now tend to go sailing with a more casual attitude about provisions, and as long as the water tanks are full, the larder can be attended to en route. This diminishes the difficulty of keeping large quantities of food cool, and around coastal waters it is generally easy to hop ashore for some marketing.

One early spring day, two of us sailed out of winter quarters planning to lie overnight in Newport, Rhode Island. The boat was outfitted, but having no plan to go cruising, there was only rice, coffee, and bourbon on board. Staples, so to speak.

The next day was so pleasing and mild that, as we started tacking up the bay, it occurred to me that the wind was just right for a reach to the Elizabeth Islands, an archipelago between the Massachusetts mainland and Martha's Vineyard. Over went the helm, the sheets rattled through the blocks, and off we went for a sail that turned into a cruise of several weeks.

Six hours later we lay in Cuttyhunk harbor, the only boat there so early in the season. It was close to dusk and cool, so once the coal stove was puffing along, chasing cold and damp, we rowed ashore to see what dinner could be drummed up. Since the little general store was not yet open for the season, it looked as though dinner might be lean.

By good chance, a young man working on his car by the roadside turned out to be a lobsterman who was happy to make an unexpected sale. He took us to the pier where his lobsters were kept in an underwater safe. As he pulled them up and opened the lid, they were flipping somersaults with their tails, their blue and green shells crackling in collision, and their massive claws pegged to prevent cannibalism.

Lobsters are good to eat, and they seem to think so too. At any rate, they wreck hell on each other when they are in close quarters. Even when they are first hatched and no bigger than a fingernail clipping they behave cannibalistically when crowded. At the lobster hatchery on Martha's Vineyard where attempts are being made to increase the overfished lobster population by raising lobsters beyond their young vulnerable stage before releasing them into the ocean, the large bowls in which they grow have circulating water in which the current keeps them slowly spinning as they float about. This way they cannot settle down and crowd each other.

Our lobsterman, whose forearms were as brawny as lobster claws, grabbed two healthy three-pounders, and we rowed off, grabbing a fistful of rockweed on the way, toward our anchor light twinkling in the distance, the sole light in the land-locked harbor.

There are many ways to cook lobster, all of them good in my opinion, for the meat is so delicious that it is difficult to do badly by it. But when boiling them, I prefer to use not more than an inch of water in the pot, for when they are not completely submerged, the shells collect less water inside and there is loss slosh on the plate.

I scooped some fresh seawater of the silent harbor, threw in the rockweed to enhance the flavor, and when the water was up to a rolling boil on the coal stove, popped in the beasts and banged on the lid. Then we talked loudly for a few seconds until their scratchings stopped. I have no qualms about killing for food. All the same, there is a tightening in the chest when any light goes out.

About ten minutes later, when the lobsters had turned to their surprising red color, they were dumped in the galley sink to drain for a minute. There was steamed rice to go with them, and some bourbon on the side. Those lobsters were the essence of lobster. It was spring, and *Jabberwock* lay snug at her mooring. As the evening temperature dropped into the thirties, the stove kept the cabins close to 80 degrees, even with the hatches open.

There are few things better to cook on than an iron Shipmate stove with an oven that is good for baking bread and roasting. But in summer weather, they provide too much heat, except for foggy evenings offshore. During the warm months, I generally relied on a two-burner alcohol stove which was mounted on sail tracks and could be pulled forward for easy access when needed, or pushed back under the galley lockers when not in use.

But in summer, few means of cooking are more pleasing that barbecuing on a lazy evening. It is a thing that many people like to do, and the vision of an anchorage of boats, each stern glowing with charcoal pots, is a comforting sight. In the old days, I used a little hibachi on the after deck, and this worked very well except that grease and charcoal invariably got on the deck, no matter how much care was taken.

Nowadays, there is a barbecue designed to attach to the stern pulpit and stick out over the water. This keeps the fire downwind and safely clear of the boat, and it has the advantage of allowing the ashes to be tipped into the water when cooking is over. Unfortunately, I have not seen one as yet designed with a removable dome lid such as home barbecues often have.

That would be ideal, because with any breeze blowing, the fire gets too fierce, while one of the best effects in such cooking is to sear meat and then add the cover so that the fire dampens down and roasts the meat as in an oven. This would also inhibit sea gulls. It seems unbelievable, but I have seen a gull swipe from a hot grill a sizzling, juicy steak. For an instant, he strugged with his theft in the air, and then dropped it into the sea about twelve feet astern. That was not a good night for dinner.

But most nights are, especially in a good harbor after a fine day of sailing. Good cooking is good for whatever ails, and the act of doing it is almost as good as the eating. So put rice in the salt cellar which keeps it dry, and keep butter on a cut-glass butter dish, for it makes things taste better that way. They break from time to time in a bad sea, but they are cheap to be had, and serve as a reminder that every meal should be a feast.

Seasickness

THE BEST OF REMEDIES is a beefsteak. That is what
Lord Byron claims in *Don Juan,* and I believe him. A
hearty meal eaten before going to sea makes for a
high and sustaining blood sugar count which offers
lots of energy for the combat to come.

It is difficult to say quite what seasickness is,
although any fool can diagnose it, especially in himself. No dread disease was ever more easily cured. A
touch of dry land will do it every time.

To put it simply in lay terms: When the human
body is repeatedly put off balance, as happens when
a ship is moving through confused waters, continuing
efforts must be made to adjust and correct balance.
As a result of these efforts, the nervous system suffers
a prolonged series of shocks, and as energy depletes,
these shocks cannot be adequately compensated for.
Fatigue and nausea set in.

The French say it best, for they call seasickness *mal
de mer,* which is to say, evil of the sea. It seems a very

Gallic concept, this putting blame on the sea, as though some dark-browed God named Vomitus were lurking in the waves.

In a way he is. For people who fear seasickness, who convince themselves they will be sick, invariably do get sick, regardless of what the seagoing conditions are. I have had people come on board for a drink in a smooth harbor and sit in a boat that was firm as any stone. As soon as a powerboat went by, throwing up a tiny wake that stirred us, they set their hands to their stomachs and begged to go ashore. This is seasickness of the head, and it leads directly to the gut. They are not joking, much.

Children do not feel this way, unless, of course, they have been primed to fear being sick. They will run around a deck under the most arduous of circumstances without ill effects, although after prolonged exposure to violent motion, they may become quite genuinely sick. At least they give themselves a chance.

There are psychological as well as physical causes for this condition, as with all illnesses. I believe that we get sick when we need to get sick, when our bodies are sending us a message to change our behavior. I also believe that sickness can come upon us, like Blake's "invisible worm that flies in the night, in the howling storm." We are not immune to an ailing world. Life is catching, even in our best moments.

But it is interesting to note that in our culture we tend to make fun of illnesses that arise from a mixture of physical and psychological causes. Drunk peo-

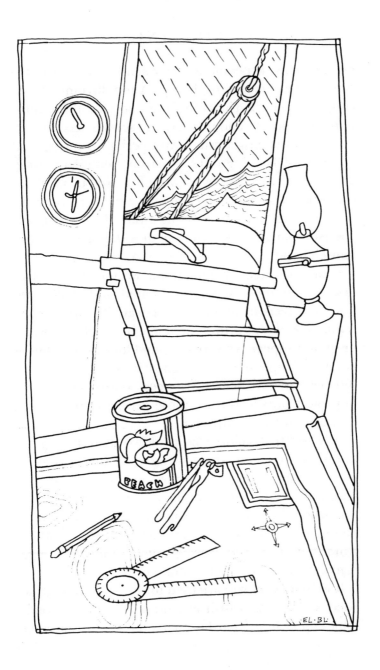

ple and seasick people are frequently the subject of bawdy jokes. In spite of their pain and discomfort, we laugh at them. Perhaps we laugh because the condition is temporary and not of dread seriousness, so our levity is not killingly cruel. And perhaps we laugh as a means of keeping ourselves from being so boring and pathetic. For there is nothing more boring than the repetitious and vulgar drunk, and there is nothing more pathetic than the inconsolable vomiting of a person hanging over the rail of a ship and wishing himself dead.

I have the feeling that when we see people disoriented in these ways, disoriented and unable to walk, it affects us in an atavistic way. We are deeply reminded of the effort mankind has made to walk upright, to speak with cogency and logic. It touches a point of shame in us to recognize how close we are to slithering on our bellies. We need control, and laugh to protect ourselves from those people who show us how close we are to disaster.

It is said that sailors who made voyages of lengthy duration on sailing ships suffered from "land sickness." During the long voyage, they had become so accustomed to compensating for the ship's motion that when they landed on some faraway beach, their inner ear continued to accommodate for the motion. Now that their feet were planted solidly on terra firma, the contrast made them feel ill.

It is all in what you are used to. I used to think that good sailors had cast-iron stomachs, and no doubt some stomachs are hardier than others, some nervous systems more naturally adept at handling shock than others. But I began to discover that good sailors are more likely to profit from cast-iron wills. They literally do not permit themselves to become sick. They know what to do about it.

For instance, the person running a boat is less likely to dwell on ill feelings than a passenger. Keeping busy helps defeat the psychological aspect that heightens the sense of sickness. When bad feelings do begin to grow, it is a good idea to get on topsides and face the breeze. An eye kept on the distant horizon is a good steadying point and helps the system accommodate shock. The important thing is not to give in and make oneself sicker, malingering in queasy misery.

Each person seems to be sensitive to a particular sea in combination with a particular point of sailing. For example, I have never had bad feelings when beating, no matter how tough the weather. But a beam reach with a big following sea tends to both lift the stern and twist it, so that two planes of motion must be compensated for simultaneously. If my energy is depleted, this point of sailing can get to me every time. I have discovered that a simple change of course quickly relieves the symptoms, and to eat a can of peaches or the like gets one ready to go back on the difficult course again.

Drinking alcohol does not help. Some people, on feeling ill, like to use booze by way of an anesthetic, and possibly for a short sail, there is something to be said for this. But for long-range sailing, alcohol is best left alone because its effect is that of a depressant and this impedes the ability of the nervous system to accommodate shock. Drinking coffee or tea is more helpful. They are nerve stimulants and offer some measure of help.

Seasickness is for me an unusual occurrence. There was a time, however, when I suffered from it quite frequently. One spring I contracted a severe case of hepatitis. When I began sailing again, my strength was more or less back to normal. I was, at any rate, able to handle sails and do whatever physical work was required to run the boat. I did tend to tire easily, especially if meals were not on schedule. My energy resources were low.

I noticed that whenever I got into any sort of a sloppy sea, sickness would set in. I used all the tricks I knew of mind over matter, and these helped, but I still got sick. My system simply was not strong enough to cope with bad motion. I happen to be one of those people who would rather do anything than vomit, so that I kept fighting my feelings and consequently seemed to feel even worse.

I developed the habit of encouraging myself to throw up as soon as I felt any strong sense of nausea. I got quite adept at it, leaving the tiller for a moment to lean over the rail, and back to the tiller before the boat had gone off course. I felt very much better, sailing on in perfect comfort until the next buildup occurred. Over the course of the summer, as my full strength returned, my resistance to sickness became normal again. It is a question of working with a problem rather than letting it defeat you.

There are, however, some people who just should not go to sea at all. A healthy young man once joined *August Moon* for a ten-day hop in the Pacific. He had not sailed before, but he had no trepidation about it, nor did he express any fear of being ill. Within an hour of our leaving port, cutting through a small chop, he began to be very ill indeed. He was also very brave about it, taking all palliative advice, eating bread, forcing down meals, taking plenty of fluids. Absolutely nothing helped. We tried giving him long watches to keep his mind occupied, even giving him antiseasickness medicine. He was ill no matter what the wind or sea conditions were. Finally we had to put him to bed, keeping him warm and feeding him fluids, while his energy and his spirits depleted until he longed for death. He said so, without a trace of wit. It was a sad tale. When we put into port, he jumped ship without saying good-bye. He simply could not get his sea legs.

Many people do very well using the various medications designed to keep sickness at bay. The problem is that they all seem to have the undesirable effect of causing drowsiness. There is little joy in a day of sailing where the head hangs ever heavy, and there is little profit on a long-distance cruise where the helmsman dozes off as he tries to follow a course. But often the pills seem to get people over a hump, especially in their fear of being sick. The pills may work effectively as a placebo where the idea of prevention is as good as a cure.

Prevention is the key to this dreary, depressing

condition. That is why I like Lord Byron's advice. Go
to sea well fed. When you feel good in your body and
secure in your soul, the chances of sickness are surely
reduced.

Storms, Hurricanes, Things That Go Bump in the Night

THE BEST SAILORS never speak of them. So, taking a place with my lesser brethren, I confess to fear and fascination both.

There is much talk, among Caribbean sailors, of being somewhere else during the summer hurricane season. Many of them do head north to the cooler waters of New England where, oddly enough, the risks of getting smashed seem to me just as likely as in the Virgin Islands. For when the great storms race across the Caribbean, if they do not head for Texas or some part of the southern coast of the United States, they tend to dash up the East Coast, whirring by New York and coming ashore so often where New England juts eastward in their path.

The great storm of 1938 and the 1954 hurricane obliterated the area. There are plaques on the walls of public buildings in Providence that mark the heights water reached. The height of a man in some places. Businesses and boats ruined, homes flooded and floated away, people and animals drowned. It is water one fears. The rush of tree-tearing wind is bad enough, but the high tides that push up estuaries combine with torrential rainfall to create the real havoc. Piers and breakwaters are overwhelmed, beaches sucked into oblivion, low-lying land flooded. At sea, the wind may knock a ship flat, but it is the waves that roll the hull and take her.

These days we can track the great storms, seeing by satellite and guessing by computer what the probability of their paths will be. There is ample warning for boats to head for hurricane holes. In the tropics, boats are tied to mango groves in nearly land-locked bays.

Warnings for New England are even better since the hurricanes will have been observed for several days in distant waters before they start their spectacular ride up the eastern coast. They cause a curious panic, these warnings, around the marinas fringing

Narragansett and other bays which are well-enough protected from general storms, but are pathetically undefended against the onslaught of water and wind that a hurricane readily musters.

The marinas are generally at the mouths of rivers leading into the larger bays. Most of them consist of floating docks that rise and fall with the tide while they are held in position by pilings. It is possible for the docks to float over the tops of the pilings when tides are hurricane high, and thereafter, everything is carnage. Boats pile up on boats, staving in hulls, jamming up like logs wherever it is they hit land.

The fact is, all one can do is make sure the insurance is paid up, and having done what is possible to secure your boat, go home and drink heavily. That helps the panic. Anything else is likely to result in injury or loss of life.

But when the warnings come, there is a rush of boat owners to the marinas. Some people beleaguer the marina operators to hoist their boats out of the water, while others purchase hundreds of feet of line with which to tie their boats down in a web that probably does more harm than good. Others strip all valuables from the cabin and store them ashore. Everywhere there is a hush of anxiety and speedy work.

Alarm, and with it, for some, excitement, leads to silly behavior. I surely sympathize with the fear of losing a boat, but not at the expense of life. That is what is likely to happen when an owner chooses to stay on board either at anchor or at the dock to ride out a storm in the hope that his presence may be of use. But the fact is that once a storm hits, the forces of wind and water are so overwhelming that human effort and strength are meaningless. One might as well place a chair before the incoming tide and command it not to approach.

It is a good idea to clear the deck of anything that might blow away or increase wind resistance. The doubling of lines and the use of good chaffing gear is vital, leaving lines slack enough so as not to tie down the boat when the water rises. Turn off the batteries, make sure the bilges are dry, and batten down the hatches. That is about it.

It is a sad thing to watch this frenzy of preparation, for what is sadder than a boat broken? The needling sense that one's best efforts are insignificant leaves a sour taste in the mouth, particularly at that last glance back towards the dock after what can be done has been done. The precious object of love left alone. Storm becomes an internal struggle.

But at any rate, we are now forewarned and can take some courage in the understanding of what is about to happen. To some degree, a thing described is a thing contained. This was not formerly the case before our sophisticated tracking stations were invented. As recently as 1938, it was not known that the great storms were in fact hurricanes that came into being down in the hot latitudes and ravaged their way north. No preparations could be made, for a hurricane approaching would give no more warning of its arrival than would a vicious line squall, a common enough phenomenon around New England waters.

I often used to wonder what it would be like to be so unprepared, not to know what monstrous force was about to envelop an entire area. How it must have at first amazed and astonished before the full weight of its power made one desperate, clawing for safe shelter. Then I found out.

Some friends had cruised with me on *Jabberwock* for a couple of weeks in Nantucket and Martha's Vineyard. It was July, and we had fair weather mostly. Fogs came and went, and our return to Rhode Island was on a bright clear day with about 25 knots of head wind. The seas were piling up as we cleared Vineyard Sound and set a course for Saconnet, so we decided to fall off and spend the/ night in the smooth land-locked harbor of Cuttyhunk Island.

The harbor was crowded with all manner of craft, so I worked upwind to the head of the fleet where there was, luckily enough, a good clear space to anchor with enough water under the keel. I always like to anchor at the head of the fleet when possible, for, provided the wind holds, the sad failings of other people do not go bump in the night.

Because the wind was holding at 25 knots, I put out the heaviest anchor I had, a 25-pound Danforth, and used as much scope as the limited space in the crowded harbor would allow. That is plenty of anchor for a 32-foot sloop. I had previously ridden out 70-knot winds safely with it. We put up the awning before settling down for a pleasant evening.

Unfortunately, just before sunset, friends on their heavy 50-foot wishbone ketch, *Stormsvalla,* arrived. They spotted *Jabberwock* and came by, urging us to

raft with them where they planned to anchor, which
was downwind near the channel separating the
anchorage from the ferry dock. They required
deeper water.

Love has its ways. We up-anchored and followed
them into deeper water. I rafted *Jabberwock* to their
port side next to the channel. We put a half-dozen big
fenders between the two hulls, tying the boats
together bow and stern and balancing them with
spring lines.

After dinner, we went to bed on our respective
boats, feeling secure in that smooth harbor. *Stormsvalla* was anchored with a 50-pound plow and plenty
of chain. As a rule, I like to clear the galley of bottles
and dishes before bedtime, especially when lying at
anchor, so that there is plenty of free space for work
should a quick start be needed. That particular night
I did not. Perhaps we had been having too much fun.

At dawn I heard a sudden splatter of heavy rain-
drops on the deck. Whoever had been sleeping in the
cockpit came hurriedly down the companionway,
closing the aft hatch. I sat up in my berth and peered
out of the forward porthole into the dim glow of
dawn. The sky ahead looked like a purple and green
bruise billowing and moving toward us.

I had never seen anything like it. I leaped up with
some alarm to check that things on deck were in
order. As I struggled into clothes, there was a drench
of rain, and even before I heard the wind shriek,
Jabberwock had heeled over 45 degrees, sending the
dishes in the galley smashing about. I got aft just in

time to see the awning flap, burst into fifty fingers of canvas, and disappear into the rain.

It was when I looked out to starboard that I felt helpless panic. *Stormsvalla* to whom we were lashed, whose heavy wooden hull was far higher than ours, was careening over us. The protecting fenders had been bounced up from between the two hulls in the ferocious motion so that our hulls were in collision. But worse was her weight crushing down on us, for, as she careened over on her side, she was actually pushing us under her, down into the water. A glance to port showed green water over the cabin windows. There was the awesome tearing of her wooden hull and the clang of pounded metal from ours. I got a glimpse of Eugene's face, his round, rimless glasses peering at me from his doghouse window, his expression utter amazement. Then he was gone as white water totally enveloped us.

There was a shadow of visibility as I looked aft, just enough to show the dinghy lying astern lift out of the water and spin on the end of its painter. Somehow the improbability of that vision helped a little. I recall thinking, Well, there goes the dinghy. And just then the cushions in the cockpit gave a heave and sailed away. I had an urge to set another anchor, but it was easy to see what an impossibility that was. My body would have been sucked off the deck and away had I ventured out.

There was something familiar in this madness, but it was not until later that I made the connection with Dorothy's dream of being inside a tornado in *The*

Wizard of Oz. Right now, my thoughts were on Eugene's anchor, and the ferry pier, and the shore, and at that instant I felt the anchor fail. The boats seemed to rear a little and began to fall back. They both straightened up, so at any rate we were no longer half-submerged, although the ugly grinding of the two hulls continued.

How vigorously the mind works in these helpless minutes. As Dr. Johnson said, "Nothing so concentrates a man's mind as knowing he will be hanged in a fortnight." At first I had been concerned with the loss of the awning, then damage to the hull, then the dinghy. Now all of those things seemed peripheral and beyond concern. The hell with the boat. It was loss of life that mattered. As far as I could tell, for the visibility was zero, we were heading directly for the ferry pier.

We hit the first piling somewhere near our chainplates. The weight of *Stormsvalla* forced us astern, so that it was her great bow that took the next blow, staving in her planks. We still could see nothing. But our motion stopped.

Then it was over. The air cleared, the wind dropped to a breeze, and we crawled in awe and shock topsides into a clearing summer morning. Only ten minutes had passed from the time of my waking until it was all over.

As I looked around, it was as though I saw in a series of concentric circles. First, we were all accounted for and safe. The boat was afloat. Eugene was hauling at fenders and he was safe. His wife,

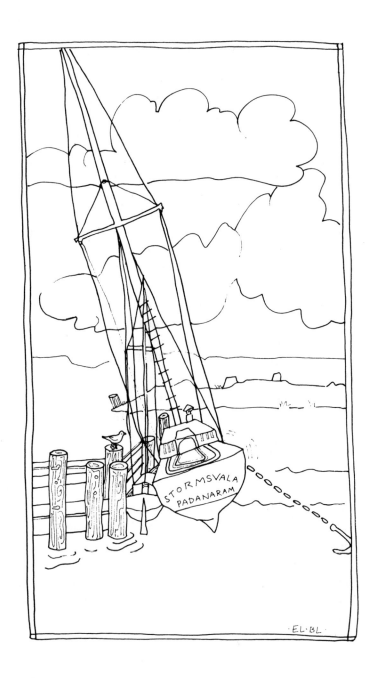

Franne, came crawling up the companionway, her long black hair soaked into tails, her eyes streaming, her hands clutching her bulging pregnant belly.

Then the boats, their bows in collision with pilings, and the pulpit of a powerboat jammed into my shrouds. Then the harbor. It was as though the hand of God had reached into that fleet of boats and strewn them without mercy about the shoreline. It was like an old print where the wind is personified as a face with bulging cheeks spewing a tempest onto tiny galleons that keel over and smash to smithereens in a rolling sea.

A 60-foot yawl had crossed our bows and tangled the pier ahead, going firmly aground in the process. A powerboat had been lifted clean out of the entrance channel to the harbor and set high and dry on shore. Three or four ketches and a couple of sloops were beached elsewhere. Boats were everywhere in collision. A dismasted sailboat went drifting by. The surface of the water was littered with oars, cushions, lost dinghies and bags of sails blown away. About two-thirds of the fleet had gone ashore, collided or dragged. There was the sound of sobbing in the air. People wandered on the pier looking frightened and shell-shocked, beginning to try and sort out the mess, think through the mess. And Franne, seeing the damage *Stormsvalla* had sustained, and looking over to the beach where grounded boats were being kedged off, shouted in anger and anguish, "Why aren't we over there?"

We were not. We got the powerboat moved aft to

take the pressure off my rigging which was sorely frayed, the upper shroud holding by one strand of steel. I feared the mast might come down before I got it jury-rigged. Then we worked to get some protection across *Stormsvalla*'s bow which was gashed as though opened with a fireman's axe.

We had the good fortune of a rising tide, so we hauled and winched, exhausted and grateful for no serious injury, until anchors were brought on board, lines were untangled and we were clear of collision. We collected oars and pillows from a distant beach. The dinghy had sunk and was kept safe that way. It was easily refloated. We cleared the pier and anchored again to count and lick our wounds. All told I had sustained about 1,000-dollars worth of damage. We juried the mast, and motored home. Only later did we discover that we had been hit by a tornado whose winds were recorded on Martha's Vineyard at well over 100 miles an hour where, in a used car lot, the vacuum created by its passing had sucked sealed windshields from the cars.

This is what happens when you hang around boats. It happens sooner or later, and the fact is that it happens often. In truth, it happens, stormy weather, calm weather, and good-sailing weather, all of them in about equal thirds. Perhaps that is why the best sailors do not speak of them, these storms. Perhaps they might frighten themselves away.

Even so, there is a profound sense of joy to this fluctuation in weather. This is especially true for the cruising sailor, for the purpose is to outfit a well-founded vessel, and then to move about the world in keeping with what the world is about and what you are about. One takes risks, of course, but against these risks are balanced the craft of seamanship, preparedness, and the concept that created the boat one sails on. This sailing about in boats is not so different from any other sort of union. Marriage, for instance, or running a business, or even the task of taking on oneself for a lifelong voyage. If the Sea and its moods suggest a metaphor for life, it is an honest metaphor. The sea is clean. It does not play games to protect itself, nor does it pretend to love you when it in fact loves another. It comes at all of us in the same way, and gives all of us the same chance to sink or swim or float. The rest is up to us.

I once thought that modern navigational aids, the good information that comes from weather stations, the vigilance and help the Coast Guard offers, made sailing a fairly dependable way of moving about. That is to say, sailors could depend on others for help when in trouble. In the coastal waters of the United States, this is often the case, but the case wavers.

People are not allowed to drive automobiles without training and licensing, and even then they are continually policed. But the fact is that any fool can buy a boat and go to sea, often endangering himself and frequently others. The carelessness with which small and large boats are managed can be dangerous and frightening.

One night, *Jabberwock* was lying at a mooring in a small fishing harbor in New England. She was moored with other boats and she was showing an anchor light. At about two o'clock in the morning, I was flung out of my berth by a sudden impact. On clambering topsides, I discovered a 26-foot boat with all sail set in collision, her sails flapping into my rigging like a moth in the dark.

I took a line from her, let her lie off my stern, and invited this specter of the night to come on board and talk about insurance matters, for my starboard rail was split, the hull somewhat buckled, and the paint wrecked.

The owner of this maunderer turned out to be someone as sensible as the chairman of a Massachusetts school board who had sailed in the dark into this tiny harbor under power with his gennie and main flying wing-in-wing. He was profounldly apologetic, saying that he had not seen me. And I must allow that sailing wing-in-wing on a pitch-black night, it is very hard to see anything that lies directly ahead. But I do not know why some people wear sunglasses indoors. Perhaps they do not wish to see.

Just as the car owner should fear collision when parked at the supermarket, any boat owner in any harbor should expect to be banged up on a regular basis, expect to have his mooring lines sliced by propellers crossing too close to his bow, expect the boat ahead to drag anchor and collide even in a flat calm, and always expect these things when he is either asleep or not on board. This is how it is, and anyone who says differently simply has not sailed enough.

In truth, when you go to sea, you are on your own.

While there are many accounts of rescue at sea, of good help given from one vessel to another, it is amazing and common to see the contrary. It lets you know what you are up against.

The passage from Panama to California is an uphill struggle in a sailing boat. There are likely to be head-winds for the entire 3,000 miles of the voyage. Motor-sailing, which is all that can be done, is always discouraging, but the alternative is to go to Hawaii, then north to the Gulf of Alaska, and afterwards reach California from the northwest. One must sail with the wind.

On such a coastal trip, *August Moon* developed engine trouble off the southern coast of Mexico. There came in her big Perkins diesel a deep, metallic clanking that none of us could diagnose, and there was an oil leakage. We reduced speed and started pouring in oil. This reduced the clanking, but didn't stop the oil leak so that the oil supply was soon exhausted. Thereafter the clanking became very loud indeed. Fearful of ruining the engine, we turned it off and put up sail, our hopes of limping into Aca-pulco under power abandoned.

There were light airs moving, just from the direction we wished to go in, so there was nothing for it but to tack out to sea, away from the coast, in the hope of finding more wind there. After three, hot, wallowing days we had made perhaps fifty miles, and then we found ourselves becalmed utterly.

There we sat, no sight of land, nor cloud, nor wind, while the big Pacific rollers tipped us over to port and

rolled us back to starboard. The sails banged and slat-
ted. The rudder rattled on its pinions. The sun at
noon stood directly overhead and beat down on us
until the varnish blistered and our brains began to
coddle. Our water supply was low and we were dan-
gerously low on food. A little breeze moved through
at sunset and again at dawn, but days were still and
without motion except for the sickening roll of the
boat from gunwale to gunwale.

A freighter appeared on the horizon one afternoon. Its course looked as though it would come quite
close to us, within a quarter of a mile, as it turned out.
We debated about asking for help, and tried to contact the freighter on the radio, but without success.

Perhaps it was that frustration, and the accident of
her being so very close to us in the middle of
nowhere, made us decide to send up a distress flare.
We waited until she was at her closest point of passage
before launching the flare. Up it went, its frothy red
trail cutting into that still, azure sky. There was nothing else to see against the wide, blank horizon.

The freighter steamed on, the black scarf of her
smoke lying straight behind her. We sent a second
rocket burning up, but still she did not alter course.
We waved, and could even see figures on the deck
who seemed to wave back, as though we had put on
this aerial display for their amusement. She crossed
to the horizon and disappeared.

These were no desperate straits to be in. Perhaps
we were not warranted in sending up a distress signal
simply to beg oil from them. But they had no way of

knowing our predicament. It could have been that we had a gravely ill man on board or the like. In any event, sail on she did without altering course by as much as a degree.

We slumped down, disconsolate, never more aware of how alone it can be to go to sea, hoping for an evening breeze. The hot, heavy days wore on.

When a breeze came it seemed miraculous, a rain squall that approached from behind, sweeping up across the unruffled rolling sea. *August Moon* seemed to purr along, the sheets wonderfully taut and straining, the happy creak and knock of blocks. The breeze was perhaps twenty knots, and with it came a tropical drench of rain so dense one had to wipe one's face to breathe. We took buckets and quickly filled them from the waterfall that cascaded off the mainsail. When the water supply was sufficiently replenished, we tore off our sopping clothes and took warm shower baths in the soft water that streamed off the sails. The days of sweat and caking salt on sore skin fled away.

Then it was gone. As quickly as the squall had arrived, it passed and dropped us. The mainsail fell flat, the gennie collapsed and sagged on the forestay. Our spirits sagged, but we were heartened by some progress made in the right direction.

Curiously enough, another squall caught up with us, and then a third. Each one of them sped us along in drenching rain for perhaps twenty minutes before escaping us, letting the boat settle limply back into the water. The squalls seemed to be moving in a circular pattern, although that was difficult to ascertain for the horizon was crammed with clouds. It was, at any rate, clear that our calm was over.

Dinner was served, and as we sat in the cockpit eating, yet another squall pushed towards us. This one did not come from behind, but rather from starboard. It was blacker than the previous ones. As we watched it swing in, there was some talk of reducing sail. Just as that decision was made, it hit us.

The ketch was sitting upright without any way on her. In about three seconds she was pushed nearly 45 degrees. A few seconds more, dinner, plates and all, went overboard as she heeled on over, desperately working to transfer the terrible pressure on her sails into forward motion. She could not do it. The mizzen shrieked and blew into tatters. The main and gennie burst several seams. Still the mast head went down and over. The three of us had leaped up to starboard, hanging from the stanchions as she went flat, our feet flailing in air for a toehold as the deck became vertical.

She lay there, her sails in the water, like a horse cast, too frightened to struggle. She was like a thing beaten, until that first ferocious gust lessened, and then she slowly began to raise herself up, the tatters of her sails blowing, and push into forward motion, the port deck still burdened with green water.

We got the sails off her. It was an effort that required the three of us to work jointly on each sail, for the pressure of wind was so great that we were almost lifted off our feet at times, and the slides on the main seemed welded to the track.

That first embittered squall lifted sheets of water off the smooth ocean surface so that we seemed to be moving over blowing snow. How quickly, even with the wind easing a little, waves began to build, their crests whipped into flying spray. At least we could set a course for Acapulco, and after so many days of calm, we wanted to take advantage of it.

Rather than lie and labor, we put up a staysail. Just those few square feet of sail allowed us to reach close to six knots. It was my watch. I would have dearly liked to be tucked below, but instead I was stuck at the helm in foul-weather gear while the storm and the night closed in.

Wind and pelting rain steadily increased over the next hour. The seas were building, but on a reach we were taking them under our quarter so that they were not uncomfortable. The boat fairly sped along, getting up toward hull speed, while the alarming wind was steady. I had the feeling that this was just one more storm to sail through when another vicious squall seemed to blast through the storm we were already in. The staysail sheet parted, and the sail flew out with a roar, with such a snap that I feared the forestay had failed.

Jim and Roger were both in their bunks below, but they felt the shudder of the hull as the sheet parted, and guessing what had happened, came naked topsides, dragging with them the heavy storm triangle.

The two of them struggled up onto the foredeck and rescued what was left of the staysail, intending to replace it with the stormsail. I got a glimpse of the sail coming down when something hit us like an explosion.

Under bare poles, the boat was knocked almost flat again. The sea was so whipped and churned that the entire hull was covered in flying water. It was as though *August Moon* were a submarine, sailing through a white night. The spray drove with such bite that I could not stand the pain of it, even though I was protected by foul-weather gear. I had to lie down in the cockpit, yelling to the foredeck that the others should come aft, but my voice was whipped away downwind before it reached even my own ears.

It seemed, as I lay there, the crests of waves breaking over us, the boat careening madly through this tempest, that there was no way the other two men could survive on that foredeck. They had to have been swept overboard, and there was nothing I could possibly do. The engine was dead. I could not, nor would I have dared, try to turn the boat into such weather. Visibility was zero, and when I gasped for air, the wind seemed to suck the breath from my lungs.

I thought of their naked bodies tumbling through that dreadful sea. Then I thought of myself, alone, helpless, terrified, being driven by this monstrosity of storm towards the Mexican coast. There was nothing to do. There was absolutely nothing to do, except lash myself to the tiller so as not to be swept overboard.

I do not think I considered anything else. There was just a numbness and the hope that *August Moon* would carry through this terrifying sea. It was clearly all up to her for now. Her big, buoyant stern kept bearing up as the waves tore at her quarters, and she staggered forward.

For about fifteen minutes, this vicious spume and wind enveloped the boat before relaxing a little. Jim and Roger came crawling on their bellies, wrapped in sails for protection, down the starboard deck. I was neither surprised nor happy to see them. Just numb. "I thought you were overboard," I said. "Lash the tiller and let's get below," Roger replied. We did.

That night was not wonderful. *August Moon* kept her starboard quarter to the seas as she moved at perhaps four knots under bare poles. The seas kept increasing in size while the wind held at somewhere over 70 miles an hour. The motion of the seas breaking over us and rolling under us was so extreme that we had to wedge ourselves on the main saloon berths with feet pressed against the table top just to keep from being thrown about the cabin.

Our main concern lodged with the doghouse which was large and had big glass windows. As the seas crested and broke over us, the doghouse took a heavy beating, and should it have carried away, we would surely have filled and foundered. As it was, water spewed in through seams and windows each time we submerged so that we soon had water up close to the floorboards. The boat felt heavy in her struggles to ride each successive wave. With the engine out of commission, we were unable to use it to pump with the automatic bilge pump, while the hand pump was located on the deck where we did not dare go. There was nothing for it but to wait, wait and let the boat take care of us.

Thus far, *August Moon* had held her quarter to the weather. But as the wave height increased during the night, more and more waves were actually breaking over her. The pounding she was taking intensified, while the steepening profile of the waves began to make the possibility of a capsize very likely. We had to do something soon.

We considered the value of putting out a sea anchor off the bow in an attempt to head her up into the wind where she might more easily ride the waves. But we were frankly afraid that we could not bring her head up, and in the process might so expose her beam in this crashing sea that the risks would be too high. Besides, the steepness of the waves projected an image of her sitting almost upright on her stern, and that was not pleasing.

Finally, we decided it was time to risk sailing again, time to start navigating these growingly monstrous waves. They were very big indeed, but as luck would have it, and dawn approached, the wind was diminishing to somewhere around gale force. That was still a fierce blast, but after what we had seen throughout this dreadful night, it seemed plausible to sail again.

In the growing light, we crawled, weakened from strain and fear, up the companionway and into the cockpit, lugging the storm trisail with us. Down

below, we had felt as though we were on a roller
coaster, but now to see this tumult was beyond imagination. The crest of oncoming waves looked to be far
over our masthead, so far above it seemed improba-
ble that *August Moon* could lift her stern and float over
them. And once up on a crest, forward and aft lay
wallowing gray valleys. It was no sea at all, but rather
the mad fantasy of some fearful dream.

But we were in luck. The length of the waves, the
distance from crest to crest, had increased, while the
wind which formerly had broken the crest over us
had slackened. It was possible to ride up over, and
then drop into that valley without being swamped in
green water. We had suffered horrendous wind. Now
we were having horrendous seas. But we did not have
both, except briefly, at once. That is the luck that
allows survival.

With the storm trisail hoisted on the inner forestay,
a tiny thick rag of a sail, we had good steerageway,
and could set a course for Acapulco. It was my watch
again, which seemed a little unfair since none of us
had managed any sleep and the previous watch taken
had been mine. But we ran our watch schedule on
very strict terms, so that the eight hours we had huddled below were counted as watches for the other two.
We did it by the clock, and even when taken by seasickness, we expected each other to stick rigidly to
schedule. It was a way of being responsible, a way of
getting along with each other without question.

I had never sailed in such seas, nor have I ever
since. And if I can avoid it, I never shall again. It was

beyond credulity. With every wave, I simply could not believe that somehow the stern would rise so that the awesome, toppling crest could pass under us, for when we were down in a trough, the wave coming at us from astern looked like a straight, solid wall that would tumble us into oblivion.

At one moment, a wide gray horizon was visible, while a few seconds later only walls of water ahead and behind could be seen. As we sped down the face of a wave, the boat really raced toward the trough until the huge and heavy *August Moon* began to surf.

This is an alarming happenstance. As a boat moves through the water, her bows cleave the water ahead which then moves smoothly around her curved lines and tumbles as it reunites at her stern. The longer the water line the greater the hull speed of a given boat. But when a hull moves beyond this theoretical speed, the smooth flow of water is disturbed. It is as though the tumble of water at her stern creeps forward so that her length lies in confused water. Steering ability is lost, while the boat ceases to carve a clean line through the water.

In this instance, with *August Moon* surfing down the wave face, she seemed to rise out of the water and push over the surface. The risks of her broaching and falling athwart the wave were keen. Had she done that, she might have been rolled and capsized when she was broadside to the wave. The other risky aspect was her speed. For as she came tearing down the wave and reached the trough, she was dependent on the buoyancy in her bows to pick her up when they slammed into the horizontal water in the trough. There are many stories of boats that cascade down the face of a wave and keep going at the bottom. Straight down.

The important action to take under such conditions is to slow the boat down, either by reducing sail or dragging lines, pillows, bedding, any impediment, behind her. Once below hull speed, steering is possible and broaching can be avoided. It also eases the work the bows must do to lift her out of the trough.

We did not want to reduce sail, for the tiny flap of canvas let us take a good course. But these were parlous conditions, so we prepared to drag line behind. Then the wind dropped by perhaps twenty knots. We soon stopped the terrifying waffling down the wave and started sailing again.

It was at this point we felt, for the first time, we really had chance of making it safely to port, when we discovered we were on a collision course with a Japanese freighter. She was coming right at us from the direction of Acapulco, pushing straight into those monstrous seas. Her bows would rise a little before dipping like a porpoise into the wave so that her entire deck back to the bridge was submerged. Then she pushed through, the wave falling off her. It was an impressive sight.

I wondered why she chose, as I would not have, to put out to sea that day, tripping through the tail end of a hurricane. But she had lots of power, and she seemed in her dramatic progress to have a control I surely did not feel. Since she was doing so well, I expected her to alter course a little to give us room to fall under her stern.

Instead, when she spotted us, she made the collision course we were already on the more pernicious by sailing even closer. We were running before on the starboard tack, and by right of that and the fact that we were a tiny storm-tossed boat, I thought that surely steam would give way to sail. As she pointed closer to us, I considered trying to head to starboard and cross her bow, but there was not room, and I feared running across the face of the wave and capsizing.

I kept expecting her to give way, hoping she would, for I did not wish to jibe under these conditions. Even though we had little sail up, the rigging might fail in this wind, and were I to time it wrong, we might broach. But she did not give way. I held course as long as I dared. Long enough to get close enough to see her crew, safe in the dry comfort of the bridge, taking pictures of us in our plight. There was nothing for it but to jibe. There was a shock that shuddered through the keel. But we made it, and went skittering off to port down the great sloping wave surging behind us.

It amazed me then, and it amazes me now, that a ship would be so thoughtless as to force a small boat into such a maneuver under such circumstances. But they did. They wanted their snapshots, it seems.

We flew under her stern, and just about then managed to pick up a radio signal from Acapulco. The wind steadily diminished and the seas diminished over the next few hours. We ate between us two cans of cling peaches whose sweet, sugary juice is easy on queasy stomachs and good for quick energy.

By the time we sailed through the gate into Acapulco Bay where the hotels were shining in luxurious sun, we were close to becalmed again. The three of us were very tired, from fear as much as exertion, but we made the effort to clear the decks, coiling line, washing off the worst of the caked salt. As Eric Hiscock says, a good sailor should always come home from a storm as though he had been out for a Sunday sail. We did our best.

But the boat felt tired under us. She looked grubby also. We had sailed so far that the paint was wearing from her waterline, and the varnish, as always, needed work. We ghosted over to the yacht club and dropped anchor. Friends who were expecting us rowed out with a bottle of champagne. We were long overdue, and they had knowledge of the previous night's weather which had done much damage in Acapulco, so they feared we were lost.

We fell asleep for a few hours, and I, thinking that I never wanted to go to sea again, thought of Ulysses. When he returned from his desperate voyages, he took an oath never to go to sea again. He took an oar in his hand and walked inland. When he reached a village where the inhabitants asked what he carried in his hand, he threw down the oar, and settled there for the rest of his life.

Fog

IT HAS TO DO WITH the heart, and then vision, and
only in the third instance is it a phenomenon where
warm air chills over water until its dew point is
reached, so forming tiny beads of moisture in the air.
It blinds.

I am in it now, sitting on the lip of the surf in California, waiting for a wind change that will drive it off
and let the sun through. There has been a week of it,
as happens when the summer weather arrives, when
warm air wafts over the cool current that flows along
the mid-coast. This fog is high, only occasionally
drifting across the sand where the warmth from an
invisible sun burns it off, only occasionally touching
the lazy spill of the surf.

A little way inland, where the mountains raise the
air up with warm vectors from the land, it disappears.
The valley leading up to the Ojai is clear and sunny.
The ranges of mountains there that set their silhou-
ettes one upon the other carry their own mist. Per-

spective disappears. The world up there becomes flat like a pre-renaissance painting when things in their confusion were amply clarified by simple and rigorous belief. It is not that way for us.

Twenty miles to sea, the Santa Barbara Islands are surely there, even though invisible. The chart is clear on such matters. What matters is knowing they are there, trusting where others have been, guarding information, looking out if one is sailing.

This California beach, even though a westerly one, faces south. At a glance, the California coast seems to run from north to south, but in its irregularities, often it does not. And for the past two days all the birds I have seen have been flying toward the west, which seems north. Gulls, pelicans, and a quickwinged flock of shearwaters, perhaps a hundred of them, dipping into the tide with their beaks, as they followed a school of anchovies. They were going west also. It might be good to know what these things mean, but it is so hard to see.

Dismal to be in fog, and dismal that it persists so often in the best days of the year, summer, when things grow apace and sailing ought to be at its best. It would be nice to think that as time passes one could see more clearly, that a wind change, like getting up well rested in the morning, would blow the fog away and allow for a new vision. The fact is, however, that the fog comes and goes, and although it is rarer in winter, there is no guarantee that it will not set then, even when unexpected. In the deepest severity of winter, up in Maine, for instance, sea smoke occurs. This is a type of fog drifting on the surface of the water to the height of a masthead. It blinds the scallop fishermen, even though the air just above is crystal clear. But it makes navigation as difficult as summer fog, and it is bitter cold.

There is nothing for it but to learn to live with fog, to sail in it when possible. This is especially true on the East Coast where fog banks so often lie on the water just beyond where bays and inlets lead into the cold Atlantic. A good day sail can be had by sailing inland, but to get anywhere that really matters, to clear Newport and reach the offshore islands, to run across Penobscot Bay in Maine and shelter close to Vinelhaven, one can wait and hope for a clear day or take chances and sail through the fog.

I took courage once after a week-long fog that had us bottled up in Newport. It had been frustrating because the fog was very thick, but each day at noon it seemed on the point of disappearing. In fact, what it did was to slide about a half-mile off the coast and then flow back in. Several boats decided to chance the passage, and we went in their company down the East Passage of Narragansett Bay and into the fog.

We had all set courses for Brenton Tower which stands about an hour sail beyond Newport, the tower that welcomes boats sailing the transatlantic races with its sound and familiar radio bleeps. We moved in parallel, each boat with a lookout posted on the bow. What visibility there was came down to perhaps thirty murky feet. To either side of us, there was the faintest shadow of a boat, and the muffled splashes of hulls sloshing through the glassy waves.

Sounds came from unanticipated angles, from behind when the nearest and barely visible boat was ahead, for instance. Fog does strange things to shouts, or the moan of distant foghorns. They twist in the cotton air and make their own confusions, like people of goodwill giving advice. It is hard to tell from what direction their voices speak.

We got a brief sight of Brenton Tower which was a relief, a promise that something stable really did exist. From there we set a course directly for Buzzards Tower near the entrance to Buzzards Bay, planning to reach Cuttyhunk Island before sunset. The boats we had accompanied set different courses towards Block Island and Long Island Sound. As we went about, they disappeared without our seeing them go. When the sheets were slackened into a reach, they were gone into the white silence.

When it is not possible to see, other senses prick up. One begins to listen more intently, to hear what might not normally be heard. A can rolling in a galley locker becomes a distraction. The quivering of the gennie's luff is a continual sound that one listens around. The thick, damp air moving by has its own heaviness of sound that dryer air moving at the same speed does not. There is a heaviness of breath that fills the ears as though one were trying to cipher sound underwater, or listening to an artificially produced "white noise."

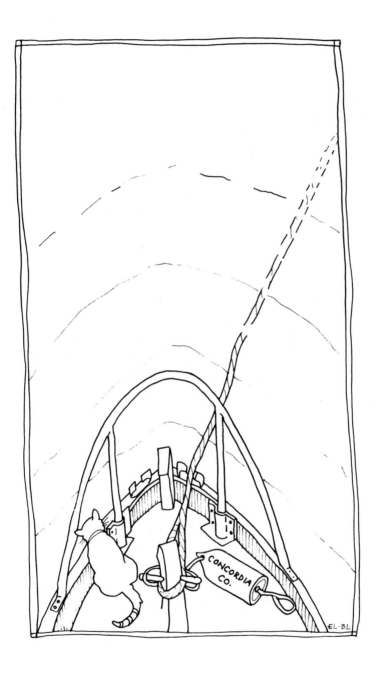

One feels the boat's motion in more subtle ways also. Irregularities in the rise and fall of her motion may mean a drift off course, or a change in current or wave pattern. It is subtle and intense, like learning to touch a stranger.

One listens and listens—for the dolorous sound of a distant bell, for the muted voice of a horn, for the flap of a wave. It seems like a form of chamber music where each player listens to his own sound and intonation while opening wider and wider the ear to hear accompanying instruments, to be one with them, in tune with them, above all to avoid collision. To dream through an inner ear.

We are in shipping lanes. Freighters that pass through the Cape Cod Canal head toward Buzzards Tower, and then to Brenton Tower if they are bound for New York. What would one hear of them in this fog? The dark throb of a massive engine? The spinning hiss of a bow wave? It is so hard to know when the fog warps sounds so that what is ahead may seem to be aft, and what one thinks to hear may be mute. Always there is the black, overwhelming vision of a monstrous iron bow cutting into the small circle of light in which we sail. The deck can be seen, the shrouds and pulpits can be sharply seen. The dinghy jostling behind like a playful and poorly trained puppy on its leash is quite distinct. That is the size of our small circle of vision, and the tangents that fly off it are fluffy and indistinct.

It is only possible to see what you can see, to move on within your own small circle of sight which will move along with you as you keep careful watch. What are the alternatives? To sit in a safe port and watch the boat corrode? To lounge around and spend money or drink? To become bored and complacent with a half-hearted ritual of day leading into night? There is fog in all of us, and quite apart from being foolhardy and taking careless risks, one has to do the best one can and sail on.

That is what we do. Sail on, keeping watch to port and to starboard, continually staring through the quadrants from beam to bow and back on either side. Occasionally one glances backward, even though it is unlikely a collision will happen from a ship hurrying from behind. It is fear that follows always from behind. A backward glance, when all one sees is the fog tumbling over the wake, fog that is neither closer nor farther away than when you last looked, a glance backward keeps one conscious of the need to look ahead.

Yet with all this looking out, how soon the unexpected happens. With all the energy we have expended in gazing at this snowy air, within a flicker of inattention, or perhaps that moment in a scan when the eye was not directly focused, suddenly there is another sailboat on the reverse course we are sailing.

Like two trains passing on parallel tracks, she appears and slides by us, or did we slide by her? The beating of her sails. For a moment, her circle of light enlarges ours and we seem to be able to see twice as far. The boats are very close, shockingly close. Neither vessel changes course because it is obvious we are not on a collision course.

There are two people keeping watch from her cockpit. All of us wave, silently, as we pass only a few feet from each other. They must have been as amazed to see us as we to see them. They go by in a gauze of color which fades foot by foot to a dark, hazy shape that in a moment becomes white again. When they disappear, as they do in a minute, the oddest sense of loneliness sets in. It is as though by having come so close, and yet having been safe, we have eaten up our good chances, our luck, and have to start all over again at not being complacent, at learning to be alone.

Somehow it seems unfair that to have come near to a collision but not to have collided is no guarantee that the next encounter will not be lethal. As though nothing has been gained that can be counted certain. One has to begin all over again, to listen so very carefully to what the sounds are really saying, and not listen to what you would like them to say. The only hope is to learn, to sail on, and to do it better through having survived it before.

Sometimes the effort is discouraging. From time to time, I recall a line from a poem of mine that I based on a line from Lorca:

> What an expense of energy
> goes into loving you.
> I'm here by a river that I can't get away from.
> I'm all used up trying to keep things flowing.

I dislike what is static in that line, what is static in the person seeing himself. The whole effort is to get through the fog, to get where you are going. It is all right to sit still if you are resting, or if you are in need of taking stock and gathering energies. But it is not all right to stop, to lie down, to stay in port and not confront the fog.

When the horn from Buzzards Tower spoke to us, it was like the voice of God blaring. Where did it come from? In what direction? Were we ahead of it or behind it? Had we passed it? We could neither see nor precisely pinpoint it. We had sailed over three hours on a single course, searching in the hope that we were right. We were right, though we could not get visual confirmation. But we had bearings again, even though they were bearings that could not be seen. The noise of the horn on the huge giraffe of a tower was so raucous and alarmingly close that from there it was safe to set a new course towards Cutty-hunk. That was a comfort.

The new course was to take us alongside Cutty-hunk, and then under the lee of Penikese Island where our landfall had to be made by sight, for there were no RDF stations to guide us. On the new course, we were moving away from the traffic of shipping lanes which was a relief. Now it was up to the compass plus my calculations of time and drift, for currents wreck havoc around those particular waters. The tides flow in and out of Buzzards Bay and mingle with tides from Vineyard Sound. They set this way and that, the speed and angle of the currents altering with each hour of the tide. The last whaling ship built to sail came out of New Bedford near the turn of the century. She had only sailed a few hours when she got into thick weather in these very waters and perished on the reefs off Cuttyhunk.

In Maine, the lobstermen put out in all sorts of weather. They move fearlessly in fog which is as much their birthright as it is a curse. Often their watery territories are inherited by a son from his father, and the rights to them are disputed with malice should a stranger press on them.

Without chart or compass, they know those waters which they daily inhabit. They know how, in the thickest fog, to move from one lobster trap to another without mishap. When you ask them how they do it, they tell very little. They indicate that they have learned to listen. That is about all one can garner of their exquisite craft.

I once knew the captain of a schooner who had sailed for a decade or more in the waters of Blue Hill and Penobscot Bays. He sailed wisely in whatever weather was presented to him. He told me how he had once crewed on a windjammer for an old man who had sailed Maine waters since the turn of the century.

They made a long passage in the densest of fogs. The old man sat at the helm with his watch and his compass, and he listened. He listened for the slight change in the surge of water as it moved over ledges far beneath the surface. He knew the waters so well that he could tell one ledge from another by the sound the water made over it. He would set a course for a particular ledge, approximating where it was by dead reckoning. His watch and his sense of drift acquainted him as to when to listen most intently. When he heard the ledge he wanted, he would go about and set his new course for the next ledge.

On one tack, he had to sail right up to a sheer-faced cliff. It was utterly lost in dense fog, and there happened not to be telltale ledges near it. The old man sat with watch and compass, waiting and timing. At a certain moment, he instructed his crew to go up on the bow with a fog horn, and at a signal give a long, hard blast on the horn. As the blare of the horn faded, the sound of beating wings came through the fog. The old man threw his helm over onto the next tack.

He had sailed right up to where he thought the cliff should be, and to check his position, had used the fog horn to frighten the gulls that nested there into the air. This provided the sound he needed to verify his position and set a new course before he smashed into the cliff. That is an art form I know very little about.

But I could have used it on the final leg of our passage to Cuttyhunk. The trick was to leave the island which stretched out long in our direction to starboard, and before reaching Penikese Island, which lay ahead and slightly to port, round the far end of Cuttyhunk and enter the harbor there.

The fog had thickened. Our circle of visibility was only a little larger than the boat. The wind had dropped, so I chose to motorsail because by doing that I could keep a constant speed through the water; this aided my calculations by time, compass and drift in knowing where we were.

About fifteen minutes before our expected land-fall, I went up and stood in the bow pulpit to keep careful watch. Fog in its drifting and various ways is tiresome to look through, for its twists and puffs seem to create their own visions. What is airy becomes for a moment solid, and what is solid sneaks back into the fog as though it were air.

This staring into nothing was so tiresome that it took me a minute to recognize that we were running smack into something solid, something white and high. Then it disappeared so that I was not sure I had seen it. There it was, and there it was not, off the starboard bow, when nothing should have been there.

We quickly circled to port, shutting off the engine to listen and to get way off the boat while trying to figure out what, if anything, I had seen. White, solid, it might have been a cliff or a structure. But it was so hard to tell, for it floated away, even in my mind's eye, to a nothing that might have been an illusion prompted by the anxiety of sailing in such heavy weather.

The depth finder showed shallow water. With the engine off, a slight surge of water moving pebbles could be heard. We were either up against Penikese Island or the tip of Cuttyhunk. The timing of our last leg indicated the latter. We circled slowly, taking readings on the depth finder, and by comparing these with soundings on the chart, established with some surety that I had glimpsed the marker near the Gos-nold Monument on Cuttyhunk.

At that instant, like a gift, a funnel of clear air

moved through the fog, and there before us, like a theatrical set revealed behind a scrim, was Cuttyhunk. Its greens and browns and rocky outcrops seemed to blaze in color after the deadening and discrete cotton of fog. We had almost hit it.

It was a vital moment, fortunate as when one glimpses what another person wants from you or you from them. Here was the chance to sail on, for I was able to get an accurate sight-bearing on the final marker we had to clear to make the harbor safely. My compass had been off some ten degrees on that particular quadrant, so that the course I had laid had been the wrong course. I had calculated right but on the wrong information. Now with a sight, it was possible to use the frailing compass to sail a straight line as the thick, damp air closed in again to blind us.

We got in and anchored, exhausted now from the relief of tension. We went below to sleep, leaving the boat floating safely in her own precious circle of light.